HOW TO LET GO AND LIVE WELL

HOW TO LET GO AND LIVE WELL

A BEGINNER'S GUIDE TO MINDFUL LIVING WITH SWEDISH DEATH CLEANING AND AGING WITH GRACE (2-IN-1 COLLECTION)

INTENTIONAL LIVING

HANNA BENTSEN

Copyright © 2024 by Hanna Bentsen

All rights reserved. No part of this book may be reproduced, stored in a retrieval system, or transmitted in any form or by any means, electronic, mechanical, photocopying, recording, or otherwise, without the prior written permission of the publisher, Teilingen Press.

The information contained in this book is based on the author's personal experiences and research. While every effort has been made to ensure the accuracy of the information presented, the author and publisher cannot be held responsible for any errors or omissions.

This book is intended for general informational purposes only and is not a substitute for professional medical, legal, or financial advice. If you have specific questions about any medical, legal, or financial matters matters, you should consult with a qualified healthcare professional, attorney, or financial advisor.

Teilingen Press is not affiliated with any product or vendor mentioned in this book. The views expressed in this book are those of the author and do not necessarily reflect the views of Teilingen Press.

To those who seek a lighter existence and a richer journey through life's seasons, may this book be your guide and companion.

Live as if you were to die tomorrow. Learn as if you were to live forever.

MAHATMA GANDHI

CONTENTS

Introduction   xi

THE ESSENTIAL GUIDE TO SWEDISH DEATH CLEANING

Introduction to Swedish Death Cleaning   3
1. Preparing to Death Clean   13
2. The Process of Death Cleaning   23
3. Tackling the Big Stuff   33
4. Cleaning as You Go   41
5. Memories and Mementos   51
6. The Emotional Journey   61
7. Practical Matters   69
8. The Art of Giving   79
9. Overcoming Challenges   87
10. Life After Death Cleaning   97
    The Lasting Impact of Swedish Death Cleaning   107

THE ESSENTIAL GUIDE TO AGING WITH GRACE

Embracing the Golden Years   117
1. Health and Wellness: The Foundations of Vitality   127
2. Relationships and Social Connections   137
3. Personal Growth and Lifelong Learning   147
4. Financial Security and Planning   157
5. The Art of Adaptation: Embracing Change   167
6. Self-Care and Independence   177
7. Leisure and Exploring New Horizons in Retirement   187
8. Health Challenges and Medical Care   195

9. The Digital Age: Staying Connected and Informed	205
10. Aging in Place: Making the Most of Your Home	215
Closing Thoughts and Reflections	223
Epilogue	231
Your Feedback Matters	233
About the Author	235

INTRODUCTION

Welcome to "How To Let Go and Live Well," a book that will guide you through purposeful decluttering and transform how you view life's later years. Through its pages, I invite you on a transformative journey to embrace the essence of living with intention. At the heart of this 2-in-1 collection is the understanding that life, with all its ups and downs, is a series of moments to be cherished and lessons to be learned.

The first volume, "The Essential Guide to Swedish Death Cleaning," explores the Swedish practice of döstädning, or death cleaning. This book illuminates a path to minimalism that transcends the physical act of decluttering, offering a way to sift through the layers of your life and legacy with mindfulness. It is a compassionate guide to creating space in your home and life and forging a deeper connection with your history and future.

Complementing this journey of letting go is "The Essential Guide to Aging With Grace," which celebrates life's golden years and challenges the stereotypes accompanying them. This volume champions the vibrancy and opportunities of later life, offering wisdom on how to thrive with vitality, purpose, and joy. It redefines

INTRODUCTION

what it means to age gracefully, encouraging you to view this stage of life not as a slow descent but as a rich opportunity for growth and fulfillment.

"How To Let Go and Live Well" encourages you to reflect on the possessions, relationships, and values that shape your life. It is for those who seek to live more intentionally, to declutter not just their physical spaces but also their minds and hearts. I hope it empowers you to release the past with gratitude, embrace the present with joy, and approach the future with confidence.

This collection offers a holistic approach to living well. It is an invitation to honor your life's journey, celebrate your achievements, and prepare a legacy of wisdom and love. Let it guide you to a life with less clutter and more meaning, where every moment is cherished and every year is golden.

THE ESSENTIAL GUIDE TO SWEDISH DEATH CLEANING

HOW TO DECLUTTER AND ORGANIZE YOUR LIFE WITH THE SWEDISH ART OF DÖSTÄDNING

INTRODUCTION TO SWEDISH DEATH CLEANING

In the quiet corners of Swedish homes, a practice known as döstädning, or "death cleaning," has long been a part of life's natural rhythm. This philosophy is not merely about tidying up in the conventional sense; it is a deeper, more introspective process that intertwines with the Swedish cultural fabric. It is a deliberate and thoughtful act of sorting through one's belongings, not due to an

INTRODUCTION TO SWEDISH DEATH CLEANING

imminent sense of one's mortality, but as a courtesy to those who remain and as a way to reflect on the memories of one's life.

The essence of döstädning lies in decluttering, simplifying, and organizing your material possessions to reduce the burden on loved ones who will inevitably have to deal with these items when you're no longer around. It is a systematic and reflective process that encourages individuals to examine their lives through the objects they have accumulated, discerning what truly holds value and what can be let go.

This philosophy is not a sad or morbid affair; instead, it is approached with a sense of pragmatism and care. It is about taking control of your belongings before they become a responsibility for someone else. The practice encourages people to keep only what they love and need, making their living spaces more manageable and their lives more focused.

At its core, döstädning is about legacy—what one chooses to leave behind for family and friends. It is an opportunity to pass on cherished possessions to loved ones, ensuring that each item carries a story or a memory rather than becoming an anonymous part of an estate sale. It is also a chance to relieve one's kin from the daunting task of sifting through decades of accumulation, which can be emotionally taxing and time-consuming.

The reflective nature of this cleaning process often leads to a profound sense of self-discovery and personal history. As individuals sift through their belongings, they may find themselves reminiscing, evaluating, and even coming to terms with different aspects of their lives. It is a way to acknowledge one's journey, celebrate achievements, reconcile with past regrets, and consciously curate the narrative one leaves behind.

In embracing the philosophy of döstädning, one also embraces a minimalist approach to living, which has been gaining traction in various cultures worldwide. This minimalist approach is not about austerity or deprivation but about finding freedom and clarity by unburdening oneself from the excess that can often distract from life's true priorities.

As we delve further into the origins and cultural significance of Swedish death cleaning, we will uncover how this practice is a practical approach to household management and a deeply ingrained societal norm that reflects the Swedish ethos of simplicity, functionality, and thoughtfulness.

Origins and Cultural Significance

The pragmatic practice of Swedish death cleaning, or 'döstädning,' is a hybrid of the Swedish words for death ('dö') and cleaning ('städning'). This methodical approach to downsizing and decluttering one's possessions is deeply embedded in Swedish society, reflecting a thoughtful consideration for one's mortality and the impact it has on those left behind.

The origins of döstädning can be traced to a common-sense approach to living that values simplicity and practicality. In Sweden, there is a cultural inclination towards not burdening others with one's belongings after passing away. This ethos extends beyond cleaning and household management; it is a philosophy that intertwines with the Swedish concept of 'lagom,' which translates to 'just the right amount.' It is about finding a balance in life, not accumulating more than one needs, and keeping only those things that serve a purpose or bring joy.

Swedish death cleaning is not just a practice reserved for older people or those contemplating the twilight of their lives. It is a lifelong process that encourages individuals to regularly evaluate their possessions and consider each item's value and relevance. It is about creating a comfortable and orderly living space that reflects

INTRODUCTION TO SWEDISH DEATH CLEANING

one's current life phase without excess material goods that can often lead to physical and emotional clutter.

The cultural significance of this practice extends beyond personal benefit. It is an act of kindness and consideration for family and friends. By systematically reducing one's belongings, individuals spare their loved ones the daunting task of sorting through a lifetime's worth of possessions. It is a final gesture of thoughtfulness, ensuring that the burden of material things does not overshadow the memories shared.

Moreover, Swedish death cleaning resonates with the concept of environmental consciousness. It encourages the repurposing, recycling, and thoughtful disposal of items, aligning with a broader commitment to sustainability and mindful consumption. This aspect of the practice embodies the importance of living responsibly with a consideration for the wider community and the environment.

The origins and cultural significance of Swedish death cleaning reflect a holistic approach to life and death. It is a practice that acknowledges the transient nature of existence and the importance of living a life that is both meaningful and considerate of the legacy one leaves behind. As we explore the interplay between mortality and materialism, we'll discover that döstädning is more than a cleaning method—it is a pathway to a more deliberate and intentional way of living.

Understanding Mortality and Materialism

When we ponder the inevitable journey each of us will take toward our own mortality, we come to realize that while our lives are transient, the material possessions we accumulate seem to outlive us, creating a silent legacy of our existence. This realization is at the heart of Swedish death cleaning, which encourages us to examine

INTRODUCTION TO SWEDISH DEATH CLEANING

our relationship with the objects we own and question what we wish to leave behind.

As we embark on this journey of decluttering with the end in mind, we are engaging in a process that is as much about introspection as it is about organization. It is a systematic approach that allows us to sift through the layers of our materialism to distinguish between what is truly valuable and what merely occupies space. This practice is not about eradicating memories or severing emotional ties but about curating them with intention and care.

The concept of materialism here is not to be frowned upon or dismissed as inherently negative. Our possessions, after all, often serve as tangible milestones of our life's journey—souvenirs from travels, gifts from loved ones, or heirlooms passed down through generations. Each item can hold a story, a memory, or a piece of our identity. However, in the context of Swedish death cleaning, we are prompted to consider the weight of these possessions, both literal and figurative, and how they might burden those we leave behind.

This reflective process is not hasty; it is methodical and can be intensely emotional. It asks us to confront our mortality and to make decisions about our belongings that reflect our final wishes. It is an act of kindness and consideration for those who will one day sift through what we've left, a way to ease their load and potentially spare them the arduous task of deciding what to keep, discard, and treasure.

In this light, Swedish death cleaning intertwines with the philosophical, urging us to ponder the impermanence of life and the permanence of the objects we leave in our wake. It is a deliberate, thoughtful process that aligns our external environment with our internal values, ensuring that our material possessions serve a purpose beyond our own tenure.

Next, we will explore how this practice brings peace of mind to the individual engaging in it and acts as a sincere gesture of love

INTRODUCTION TO SWEDISH DEATH CLEANING

and respect for those who will carry on after us. The benefits of Swedish death cleaning extend beyond the individual, fostering a sense of continuity, connection, and care for the collective well-being of our loved ones and the memories we choose to leave with them.

Benefits of Death Cleaning for You and Your Loved Ones

In contemplating the inevitability of mortality, we uncover a heartfelt truth: the possessions we accumulate over a lifetime hold meaning both for us and for those we will one day leave behind. Swedish death cleaning is a compassionate and practical approach to addressing this reality. It is a process steeped in thoughtfulness, aiming to ease the burdens our material belongings might place on our loved ones after our passing.

The benefits of this practice are manifold. For the individual, death cleaning serves as a reflective exercise, a way to review one's life through the lens of physical objects. Each item we choose to keep or part with can reflect a cherished memory, a lesson learned, or a story we wish to pass on. This intentional sorting and decluttering can lead to a sense of peace and fulfillment, knowing that our material legacy will reflect our true values and the essence of what we hold dear.

Death cleaning can be a cathartic release from the often-unnoticed weight of possessions. As we sift through the layers of our material history, we may find ourselves unburdened by the past, free to live more fully in the present. The space we create in our homes can lead to a clearer mind and an environment that nurtures well-being. It is about making room not only in our closets and drawers but in our hearts and minds for new experiences and joys.

For our loved ones, the benefits of death cleaning are equally significant. In the wake of loss, sorting through a lifetime's worth of

INTRODUCTION TO SWEDISH DEATH CLEANING

belongings can be emotionally and physically overwhelming. By undertaking this process ourselves, we can spare our family and friends the daunting task of making difficult decisions about our possessions without our guidance. It is a final act of care and consideration, a way to ease their grief and to provide them with a curated collection of memories rather than a cluttered space to sort through.

Death cleaning can also serve as an opportunity for meaningful conversations with our loved ones about our possessions and the stories they carry. It allows us to share the significance of certain items, ensuring they are understood, appreciated, and preserved if we desire. It also opens a dialogue about our wishes, fostering understanding and reducing potential disputes over material things when we are no longer there to mediate.

In essence, Swedish death cleaning is about more than simply tidying up before we depart from this world; it is a deliberate and loving preparation for the inevitable transition we all must face. It is about taking control of our legacy, ensuring that what we leave behind is not a burden but a reflection of our life's narrative, carefully edited and thoughtfully arranged for those we love. As we embark on this journey, we set the stage for a process that is as much about celebrating life as it is about preparing for death.

Beginning Your Death Cleaning Journey

As we embark on the journey of Swedish death cleaning through the chapters of this book, it is essential to approach the process with a clear and prepared mindset. This approach to decluttering extends beyond tidying up; it is a thoughtful practice aimed at simplifying your life and leaving behind a considerate legacy. To set the stage for your death cleaning journey, we will delve into some practical steps to guide you through this reflective process.

INTRODUCTION TO SWEDISH DEATH CLEANING

Begin by acknowledging the scope of the task at hand. Death cleaning is not an overnight endeavor, nor is it a race. It is a gradual process that requires patience and perseverance. Start by setting realistic goals and timelines that resonate with your own circumstances. Whether you tackle one room at a time or categorize items by their emotional and functional value, the key is to proceed at a comfortable and manageable pace.

Next, gather the tools and materials to support you throughout this journey. Arm yourself with boxes, labels, and cleaning supplies. These will serve as helpful aids in your quest to sort, organize, and, if necessary, part with possessions. Consider also keeping a notebook or digital document to record your thoughts, decisions, and the stories behind certain items. This can be an invaluable resource for reflection and practicality, as it helps track your progress and the reasoning behind your choices.

As you prepare to dive into the physical aspects of death cleaning, take a moment to reflect on your intentions. Remind yourself of the benefits this process will bring to your own life and those of your loved ones. By reducing the burden of unnecessary belongings, you are crafting a clearer space and a more focused existence. You are also ensuring that your legacy is one of thoughtfulness and consideration rather than a daunting task for others to handle in your absence.

It is also important to consider the emotional journey that accompanies sorting a lifetime's worth of possessions. Some items will stir memories and emotions, and it is crucial to acknowledge and honor these feelings as they arise. Allow yourself moments of reminiscence and gratitude for the experiences and people that have shaped your life. However, remain steadfast in your resolve to make decisions that align with your ultimate goal of simplicity and mindfulness.

Lastly, do not hesitate to seek support. Whether it is the

INTRODUCTION TO SWEDISH DEATH CLEANING

companionship of a friend or family member during the sorting process or a professional's advice when appraising valuables, remember that you are not alone in this endeavor. Sharing the experience can lighten the load and provide a sense of camaraderie and shared purpose.

We will explore these moments of preparation in more detail in the next chapter. By properly preparing for the tasks ahead, you are setting yourself up for a thorough and meaningful decluttering journey. You may encounter challenges and emotional hurdles, but remember they are all part of the process, and the path you pave is one of clarity and generosity. Embrace the process with an open heart and a practical mind, and let the act of decluttering be an act of liberation and testament to a life well-lived.

Chapter Summary

- Döstädning, or Swedish death cleaning, is a reflective process of decluttering one's possessions as a courtesy to those who remain after one's passing.
- It is not a sad task but a pragmatic and caring act to control one's belongings and reduce the burden on loved ones.
- The practice is about legacy, allowing individuals to leave behind meaningful items with stories rather than anonymous clutter.
- It encourages a minimalist lifestyle, focusing on keeping only what is loved and needed. It is deeply rooted in Swedish culture.
- Swedish death cleaning reflects the Swedish ethos of simplicity and thoughtfulness, and it is not just for the elderly but a lifelong process.

INTRODUCTION TO SWEDISH DEATH CLEANING

- The practice is also environmentally conscious, promoting repurposing and recycling to align with sustainable living.
- It involves introspection and confronting one's mortality, curating possessions to reflect one's values, and easing the burden on loved ones.
- The process is gradual and requires preparation, patience, and support, ultimately aiming to leave a considerate and focused legacy.

1

PREPARING TO DEATH CLEAN

Embarking on the journey of Swedish death cleaning can be an intense and emotional process that requires a certain level of mental preparedness. It is a thoughtful and reflective act that involves sifting through a lifetime of possessions and deciding what truly matters.

Before diving into the practical aspects of decluttering, it is important to acknowledge the emotions that may surface. You may experience many feelings, from nostalgia to sadness, relief to anxiety. It is normal for memories to flood in as you handle various items, each with its own story and sentimental value. Allow yourself to sit with these emotions, to recognize and honor them. This process is as much about the physical items as it is about respecting your life and the memories you've created.

To prepare mentally and emotionally for death cleaning, start by reflecting on your intentions. Why have you decided to undertake this process? You may wish to simplify your life, provide a sense of order, or spare your family the task of sorting through your belongings. Clarifying your motivations will provide a sense of purpose and direction, making the process less daunting.

Next, consider the scope of what you will be dealing with. This is not a task to be rushed; it requires patience and thoughtfulness. It may be helpful to journal your thoughts and feelings as you go, providing an outlet for reflection and a record of your emotional journey.

Talking to your loved ones and sharing your intentions is also beneficial. Death cleaning is ultimately an act of kindness towards those you will one day leave behind. Discussing your plans can not only help you emotionally but can also provide comfort and understanding to your family and friends. They may offer support or share in the reminiscing, making the process a shared experience.

Remember, mental and emotional readiness is not about achieving a state of detachment or indifference. It is about approaching the task with a sense of peace and acceptance. It is about making deliberate choices that reflect your life, your values, and the legacy you wish to leave.

As you find yourself mentally and emotionally prepared, you may naturally progress toward creating a structured approach to your death cleaning journey. This involves establishing a plan and timeline to guide you through the practical steps of decluttering, ensuring the process is manageable and aligned with your personal goals.

Creating a Plan and Timeline

Once you've established the mental and emotional readiness to undertake the Swedish death cleaning process, it is time to focus on the practical aspects of this journey. Creating a plan and timeline is an important step that will provide structure and clarity to the task ahead.

Begin by assessing the scope of your possessions. Take a walk through your living space and make a mental inventory of the items that fill each room. Consider the furniture, the hidden items in closets and drawers, and even the keepsakes tucked away in attics or basements. This initial assessment will give you a sense of the magnitude of the task and help you estimate the time needed for each area.

Once you have a general overview, it's time to set realistic goals. Death cleaning is not a race; it is a deliberate process that may take weeks, months, or even years, depending on your circumstances and the volume of possessions to sort through. Decide on a timeline that feels comfortable for you. Some may prefer to dedicate a few hours each week, while others allocate entire days to the process.

As you create your timeline, consider the emotional weight of certain items. You may need to allocate more time to sort through personal mementos than you would for everyday household items. Be flexible and allow yourself the freedom to adjust your schedule as needed.

Next, break down your plan into manageable tasks. You might start with a particular room or category of items. For instance, beginning with clothing or books can provide a sense of accomplishment and momentum. As you progress, you can move on to more challenging categories.

It's also important to consider the logistics of disposing of items. Will you donate, sell, recycle, or discard the things you choose not to keep? Research local charities, second-hand shops, and recycling centers in advance. Knowing your options will make it easier to part with items when the time comes.

Lastly, keeping a record of your plan and timeline can be helpful. Whether a digital document or a handwritten journal, tracking your progress will help you stay on course and adjust your plan as necessary. It will also remind you of the work you have accomplished and the remaining steps.

By systematically planning your approach and setting a timeline that considers your emotional and physical needs, you can embark on a thoughtful and fulfilling journey toward a more intentional and unburdened life.

Gathering Supplies and Resources

It is essential to gather the right supplies and resources before delving into the task at hand. This preparation will facilitate a smoother transition through the various stages of decluttering and provide a sense of readiness and control, which can be particularly comforting.

To begin, you will need various sturdy boxes and bags for sorting items. These could come in different sizes to accommodate everything from books and papers to clothing and keepsakes. Labels or colored markers can help categorize these containers into groups such as 'keep,' 'donate,' 'recycle,' and 'throw-away.' This visual system will make organizing your belongings and tracking your progress easier.

Next, consider what cleaning supplies you may need for the

task. This could include cleaning cloths, dusters, sprays, and garbage bags. A clean and dust-free environment is conducive to thoughtful decision-making. Having a toolkit on hand for dismantling any furniture or fixtures you decide to part with is also practical.

In addition to physical supplies, you could also compile a list of resources that might be needed. This could include contact information for local charities that accept donations, recycling centers, and waste disposal services. You might also gather information on consignment shops, online marketplaces, or auction houses if you anticipate selling any items.

Documentation is another critical aspect of Swedish death cleaning. Ensure you have a filing system for important papers, such as wills, property deeds, and personal letters, which you may want to pass on or discuss with family members. A shredder might be necessary for securely disposing of sensitive documents that are no longer needed.

Lastly, it's beneficial to have a notebook or digital document to record your intentions for certain items, jot down memories or messages associated with particular belongings, and track your overall progress. This can be a reflective tool, allowing you to ponder the significance of the items in your life and the legacy you wish to leave.

Gathering these supplies and resources aims to create a supportive environment that will ease the physical and emotional workload of death cleaning. With everything in place, you can approach this task with a clear mind and a prepared heart, ready to make decisions that honor your life and your loved ones.

Communicating with Family and Friends

An essential step in the process is to open lines of communication with family and friends. Swedish death cleaning is a deeply personal and often emotional endeavor that affects the individual undertaking it and those around them. Therefore, it is important to approach this communication with sensitivity, clarity, and purpose.

Begin by setting aside a quiet time to talk with your loved ones. Explain the concept of Swedish death cleaning to them – the practice of mindfully organizing and reducing one's possessions to lessen the burden on others after passing. Emphasize that this is a proactive and considerate act, one that is done out of love and respect for those who will remain.

Express your desires and intentions clearly. Let them know that you are preparing for the future and seeking to create a more orderly and peaceful environment in the present. This is a time to share your thoughts on the significance of certain items, perhaps heirlooms or personal mementos, and to discuss who might appreciate or have use for them.

It's important to be receptive to their feelings and thoughts as well. They may have attachments to certain items or memories you are unaware of. This process can serve as a bridge to understanding. It can help in making decisions that honor the sentiments of all involved.

Encourage family members to ask questions and to express their preferences or concerns. Some may wish to claim certain items, while others may have practical suggestions for distributing or disposing of possessions. This dialogue can help prioritize what to keep, what to gift, and what to let go of.

Remember, this process is not about rushing or making hasty decisions. It is a gradual and thoughtful progression and also an opportunity to share stories, reminisce, and acknowledge the emotional weight that objects can carry. By involving your loved ones, you are preparing your estate and creating a space for collective reflection and understanding.

This communication can be seen as a gift in the spirit of Swedish death cleaning. It is a chance to ensure that your legacy is preserved in the way you wish and that the process of sorting through your life's collection is done with respect and consideration for those you love. It is a step towards peace of mind for you and your loved ones as you declutter with intention and grace.

The Role of Forgiveness and Letting Go

Before you begin sorting through your possessions, take a moment to stop and cultivate a mindset that embraces forgiveness and the art of letting go. The Swedish death cleaning process involves an emotional and psychological readiness to part with items intertwined with our life stories, but this is not always easy to do.

Forgiveness, in the context of death cleaning, is a multifaceted tool. It involves forgiving ourselves for the accumulation of belongings that we no longer need or may burden our loved ones after we are gone. It is a gentle acknowledgment that holding onto certain items out of guilt or obligation serves no one in the long run. We must also extend forgiveness to others who may have given us gifts or heirlooms that do not align with our current values or lifestyle. By releasing any feelings of resentment or obligation, we pave the way for a more thoughtful and intentional selection of what to keep and what to let go.

Letting go is a complementary process to forgiveness. It is the physical manifestation of our emotional release. As we sift through our belongings, we may encounter items that stir up memories of past conflicts, regrets, or unresolved issues. It is essential to recognize that holding onto these physical reminders does not change the past nor heal old wounds. Instead, by letting go of such items, we are making a conscious decision to move forward, to create space for new experiences and memories that are in harmony with who we are in the present.

The act of letting go also extends to our relationships. As we prepare for death cleaning, it is an opportune time to mend fences and express gratitude or apologies where needed. This does not mean we must keep every token of affection or every memento of a shared experience. Instead, it is about cherishing the essence of our relationships and allowing the physical items to be just that—items that do not define the depth or significance of our connections with others.

In practice, a few reflective exercises can facilitate forgiveness and letting go during the death cleaning process. Consider writing a letter to yourself or someone else, expressing the thoughts and feelings that arise as you handle each item. You do not need to send these letters; their purpose is to provide a private space for acknowledgment and release. Another method is to take a moment with each challenging item, thanking it for its role in your life, and then consciously deciding its fate—be it donation, recycling, or disposal.

Swedish death cleaning aims not to erase the past but to curate a legacy that reflects the most meaningful and loving aspects of our lives. By incorporating forgiveness and the practice of letting go, we can set ourselves up for a more meaningful and liberating death cleaning journey.

Chapter Summary

- Swedish death cleaning is a personal and emotional process that involves acknowledging emotions and reflecting on the life lived and memories created.
- Mental and emotional preparation for death cleaning includes understanding motivations, setting a purposeful direction, and patience.
- Communicating with family and friends about the process can provide emotional support and shared understanding.
- Creating a structured plan and timeline helps manage the decluttering process, considering the emotional weight of items.
- Gathering supplies like boxes, bags, cleaning materials, and a filing system for important documents is essential.
- The process aims to curate a meaningful legacy. Various strategies can help facilitate emotional release, including forgiving oneself for accumulated belongings and letting go of items that no longer serve a purpose.

2

THE PROCESS OF DEATH CLEANING

Having cultivated an intentional mindset and prepared yourself for the journey ahead, begin with the simplest tasks. This approach is practical and serves as a gentle introduction to the process, allowing you to ease into the more challenging aspects that may follow.

The first step is to identify items in your home that are the easiest to sort through. These objects often hold little sentimental value and are simply taking up space. You could begin with the miscellaneous drawer everyone has in their kitchen, filled with random utensils, takeout menus, and unclaimed keys. Or consider starting with your wardrobe, where clothes that no longer fit or have gone out of style can be the first to go. The goal is to build momentum, creating a sense of accomplishment to fuel your journey through the more sentimental items.

As you sort through these belongings, it's essential to remember the guiding principle of death cleaning: to minimize the burden on loved ones after one's passing. With each item you decide to part with, ask yourself if it will be valuable or useful to others. If not, it may be time to let it go. This process is not about discarding memories but about curating them. It's about making conscious decisions on what is truly important to keep and what can be released.

The systematic approach to starting with the simplest tasks also allows for reflection. With each item you handle, you're given the opportunity to reminisce and acknowledge its role in your life. This reflective practice is an integral part of Swedish death cleaning, as it helps in letting go of physical items and processing the memories and emotions attached to them.

Once the simplest tasks are underway and progress is visible, tackling the following category of belongings becomes easier. This gradual progression ensures that the process is manageable and that each decision is made with care and consideration. By starting simple, you lay a solid foundation for the more complex sorting that lies ahead.

Sorting Personal Belongings by Category

Having established a foundation by starting with the simplest tasks, we now transition into a more structured phase of the Swedish death cleaning process: sorting personal belongings by category.

This approach not only brings order to what may initially appear as an overwhelming task but also provides clarity and a sense of progress.

Begin by designating specific areas in your home for different categories. These categories include clothing, books, papers, household items, and personal mementos. Organizing items by category creates a visual and physical structure to guide you through the decluttering process.

When sorting clothing, consider the practicality and emotional value of each item. Ask yourself if the clothing is in good condition, has been worn recently, or holds significant sentimental value. Depending on their condition, clothes that are no longer needed or wanted can be donated, sold, or recycled.

Books, which often hold sentimental value, require a thoughtful approach. Reflect on which books have been meaningful to you and why. It may be helpful to consider whether these books would be of value or interest to others. If they are not, it might be time to let them go.

Papers can be one of the more daunting categories due to the sheer volume and the sensitive nature of the information they may contain. Start by discarding obvious items like outdated receipts, expired warranties, and old catalogs. Then, organize important documents such as legal papers, personal letters, and photographs, which may need to be kept or passed on to family members.

Household items encompass everything from kitchenware to decorative objects. Evaluate each item's usefulness and the likelihood of it being used by someone else. Items that are functional and in good condition are excellent candidates for donation or gifting.

Personal mementos are often the most challenging due to their emotional ties. While this category will be addressed in greater depth in the following section, it is important to approach these items with a balance of sentimentality and practicality. Consider which items genuinely enrich your life and which someone else might appreciate more.

Throughout this process, maintain a reflective mindset. Contemplate the life you have lived and the objects that have accompanied you along the way. This physical decluttering is also a thoughtful journey through your past, with a focus on creating a lighter future for yourself and your loved ones.

By categorizing your belongings, you create a manageable path forward in the death cleaning process. This structured approach allows you to address each category with focus and intention, making the task less overwhelming and more meaningful.

Dealing with Sentimental Items

As you sort through your belongings, you'll inevitably encounter the delicate task of dealing with sentimental items. Often brimming with personal history and emotional resonance, these objects can be the most challenging to address. They are the tangible manifestations of cherished memories, relationships, and experiences. In this process, we must tread with care, balancing respect for the past with the present and future practical necessities.

The first step in confronting sentimental items is acknowledging their emotional weight. Feeling strongly attached to personal mementos, such as photographs, letters, handmade gifts, or family heirlooms, is natural. These items often connect us with those we love and the moments that have shaped us. Recognizing the significance of these objects is crucial before any decisions are made about what to do with them.

Once we have honored the emotional significance of these items, it is time to reflect on their place in our lives moving forward. Ask yourself: Does this item still serve a purpose? Will it bring joy or utility to someone else? Is it something that I want to be part of my legacy? Reflection is a critical component of Swedish death cleaning and is especially pertinent to sentimental objects.

In this reflective process, it can be helpful to consider the concept of impermanence. Objects, much like life itself, are transient. Holding on to every item of sentimental value is neither feasible nor in keeping with the ethos of death cleaning, which is to simplify and unburden. It is about making room for the new physically and emotionally while still honoring the past.

One practical approach to managing sentimental items is to curate a selection of representative pieces. For example, instead of keeping every drawing your child ever made, you might choose a few that are particularly meaningful. This allows you to preserve the essence of your memories without being overwhelmed by volume.

Another approach is to digitize items where possible. Photographs, letters, and documents can be scanned and stored electronically. Digitizing saves physical space and ensures that these memories are preserved in a format that is less susceptible to decay over time.

For items unsuitable for digitization, consider whether they might find a second life with someone else. A piece of jewelry you no longer wear might bring a family member or friend joy. A collection of books could be donated to a library or school. In passing these items on, you give them a new purpose and extend their narrative beyond your own story.

When it comes to particularly challenging items that you cannot bear to part with but know you should, it may be helpful to involve a trusted friend or family member in the decision-making process. They can offer a fresh perspective and help you weigh the item's sentimental value against its practical considerations.

When dealing with sentimental items, giving yourself permission to let go is important. This does not mean discarding memories or relationships but consciously choosing what to carry forward. It is a process that requires time, patience, and self-compassion.

Making Decisions: Keep, Gift, Donate, or Discard

Having explored the delicate task of sorting through sentimental items, we now focus on the broader scope of belongings that populate our lives. The Swedish death cleaning process is not merely about decluttering; it is a thoughtful journey through your possessions, determining what truly matters and what can be let go. This phase—deciding whether to keep, gift, donate, or discard items—is perhaps the most critical step in the process.

To begin, establish a serene and undistracted environment. This will facilitate a clear and focused mindset, which is essential for making decisions you will be content with in the long run. Start with items that have less emotional weight. These are often easier to address and can help you build momentum and confidence in your decision-making abilities.

When considering each item, ask yourself a series of questions: When was the last time I used this? Does it bring me joy or serve a practical purpose? Could someone else benefit more from having this? Your answers will guide you toward one of four choices: keep, gift, donate, or discard.

Keep

Keep only those essential items that bring you happiness or have a designated purpose in your life. These are the things that you use regularly or that contribute positively to your daily existence. Be honest with yourself about what you truly need and value.

Gift

Gift items you no longer need but could have a meaningful second life with a family member, friend, or acquaintance. Gifting is a beautiful way to extend an item's life and share something of personal significance with others. It can be especially rewarding to pass on heirlooms or personal treasures to those who will appreciate and cherish them.

Donate

Donate items that are in good condition but do not hold significant personal value. There are many charities and organizations that can use clothing, books, furniture, and other goods to help those in need. Donating clears your space and contributes to the well-being of others and the wider community.

Discard

Throw away items that are broken, worn out, or otherwise no longer useful. This includes expired medicines, outdated electronics, and damaged goods. Disposing of these items responsibly, recycling where possible, and being mindful of the environment is essential.

Remember that Swedish death cleaning aims not to leave behind an empty home but to curate a space that reflects a well-lived life, free of unnecessary clutter. It's about making your surroundings as manageable as possible, both for you and for those who might inherit your space and belongings.

As you make these decisions, consider the practicalities of your current lifestyle and the legacy you wish to leave. Letting go can be liberating, and you craft a clearer, more intentional living space with each decision.

Once you have sifted through your belongings and made these decisions, the next step is to organize and store what remains to maintain the order and tranquility you've worked to achieve. This will ensure that your home is not only tidy but also that your cherished possessions are accessible and enjoyed in your daily life.

Organizing and Storing What Remains

Having navigated the emotionally charged waters of deciding which possessions to keep, gift, donate, or discard, you can now focus on the practicalities of organizing and storing the items that have earned their place in the 'keep' category. This is not a step to be overlooked in the Swedish death cleaning process, as it ensures that the retained items are accessible, well-maintained, and do not contribute to unnecessary clutter.

Begin by considering the space you have available. Be realistic about the volume of belongings you can comfortably store without overcrowding your living space. This might mean re-evaluating items if your available space is less than the volume of items you initially decided to keep. Remember, one of the goals of death cleaning is to create a serene and manageable environment for yourself.

Once you've confirmed that your kept items are in harmony with your space, focus on organizing them in a way that reflects their frequency of use and emotional value. Everyday items should be easily accessible, while those with sentimental value that are used less frequently can be stored in a way that protects them from dust and deterioration.

For instance, consider transparent storage containers for items you don't use daily but wish to keep visible. This allows you to appreciate these items without handling them, reducing the risk of physical damage. Labeling these containers can also be a thoughtful gesture, as it provides context and guidance for anyone handling your affairs in the future.

For documents and personal papers, create a filing system that is both logical and clearly labeled. This could include categories such as personal identification, property deeds, financial records, and sentimental letters. Ensuring these are well-ordered not only aids you in locating them when needed but also simplifies the process for your loved ones.

When storing clothing, prioritize garments that are seasonally appropriate and in good condition. Consider professional preservation methods if you have special attire that you no longer wear but wish to keep for sentimental reasons, such as a wedding dress or a military uniform. This could include acid-free boxes or vacuum-sealed bags that prevent aging and protect the fabric.

Finding a balance between aesthetics and practicality is essential for more oversized items like furniture or artwork. Suppose a piece of furniture is rarely used but holds significant sentimental value. Could it be repurposed or displayed differently to integrate it into your daily life? Artwork should be displayed in a manner that allows for enjoyment but also preserves its condition, away from direct sunlight and humidity.

Throughout this process, maintain a reflective mindset. Consider the memories and emotions attached to each item you organize and store. This journey allows you to revisit cherished moments and, in some cases, to let go of the past to embrace a more unburdened present.

Organizing and storing what remains after the death cleaning process is a deliberate act of curating your life's collection, tidying up your living space, and ensuring that what you leave behind is a true reflection of your legacy.

Chapter Summary

- The Swedish death cleaning process can begin with simple tasks, such as sorting through items with little sentimental value, to build momentum for tackling more sentimental belongings.
- Items can be sorted by category, including clothing, books, papers, household items, and personal mementos, with a focus on what to keep, gift, donate, or discard.
- Sentimental items should be addressed with care, considering their emotional significance and whether they should be kept as part of one's legacy or let go.
- Practical strategies for sentimental items include curating a selection of representative pieces, digitizing where possible, and involving others in the decision-making process.
- Decisions on belongings can be made by asking yourself if they bring joy, serve a purpose, or could benefit others, leading to keeping, gifting, donating, or discarding.
- When organizing and storing kept items, consider space availability, frequency of use, and emotional value, with a focus on accessibility and maintenance.
- The final goal is to create a serene and manageable living environment, with organized belongings that reflect a well-lived life and intentional legacy.

3

TACKLING THE BIG STUFF

In Swedish death cleaning, we confront the physical bulk of our existence: the furniture and oversized items that fill our spaces and, in many ways, define the backdrop of our lives. These pieces have supported us, literally and figuratively, and deciding their fate requires a blend of practicality and sentimentality.

As you approach the task of sorting through your furniture, it's essential to start with a clear plan. Begin by assessing each item for its current use and emotional value. Ask yourself: When was the last time this piece was used? Does it hold significant sentimental value, or is it simply occupying space? Be honest in your appraisal, as this will guide you in making thoughtful and decisive decisions.

Once you've evaluated your furniture, consider the options for each piece. Some items may be heirlooms or hold sentimental value for family members. Reach out to them to gauge their interest—this ensures that meaningful pieces are preserved within the family and helps in the letting-go process, knowing these items will continue to be cherished.

For furniture no longer needed or wanted, selling or donating can be a suitable path. Items can be sold through various channels, such as online marketplaces, consignment stores, or garage sales. When pricing, be realistic about the item's condition and market value. Remember, the goal is not necessarily to make a profit but to find the furniture a new home where it will be utilized and appreciated.

Donating is another avenue, particularly for items that may have low resale value but are still functional. Many charitable organizations welcome furniture donations, and some will even arrange for pick-up, easing the logistical burden. This option clears space and contributes to a good cause, aligning with the thoughtful ethos of death cleaning.

Disposal may be the only option for those pieces that are beyond repair or unsuitable for donation. However, it's essential to do so responsibly. Check with your local waste management services for guidelines on furniture disposal or recycling programs that may be available. Some materials, such as wood or metal, can be recycled, reducing the environmental impact of your clean-out.

Each item you part with has been a part of your story, and it's natural to feel a sense of loss or nostalgia. Allow yourself to experience these emotions, but also embrace the liberation that comes with making space—both physically and emotionally.

By systematically addressing the furniture and oversized items in your home, you create an environment that is more manageable and aligned with your current life stage. This thoughtful reduction of your belongings serves as a gift to your future self and loved ones, encapsulating the true spirit of Swedish death cleaning.

Electronics and Appliances

Now, we focus on the electronics and appliances that have served us throughout the years. Often brimming with modern convenience, these items can be surprisingly laden with memories and attachments. Yet, they demand a unique approach when it comes to decluttering.

Firstly, assess the electronics and appliances you possess. Consider their utility, condition, and the likelihood of their use in the future. Begin by gathering all such items from around your home into one area. This consolidation allows for a clearer perspective on what you have and what truly requires attention.

Reflect upon each item thoughtfully. That old radio might not have been turned on in years, but perhaps it was a gift from a dear friend. The blender, now gathering dust, might remind you of culinary adventures past. Acknowledge these memories and recognize that holding onto the physical item is not always necessary to preserve the sentiment.

Once you have decided which items will not accompany you further, consider their potential for a second life elsewhere. Electronics and appliances in good working order might find a welcome home with family members and friends or through donations to charity shops and organizations that specialize in providing essential items to those in need. This not only extends the useful life of the item but also contributes to a cycle of generosity and sustainability.

Responsible disposal is vital for items that are no longer functional or have become obsolete. Many electronics contain materials that are harmful to the environment if not handled correctly. Research local e-waste recycling programs or facilities that can ensure these items are disposed of in an environmentally friendly manner. Some manufacturers and retailers also offer take-back programs for their products, which can be a convenient option.

While sorting through your electronics and appliances, you may encounter cords, chargers, and accessories whose purpose has long been forgotten. These can quickly become clutter without us even realizing it. Gather these miscellaneous items and attempt to match them to their counterparts. Unpaired or unneeded items can be disposed of with the same care as electronics, often through the same recycling channels.

As you work through this section of death cleaning, remember to keep records of what you dispose of, especially if you discard items that may contain personal data. Wipe hard drives, perform factory resets on devices, and remove any SIM or memory cards. Your aim is to ensure that your personal information remains secure even as your possessions move on from your life.

Books, Media, and Artwork

Books, media, and artwork often hold significant emotional value and can tell the story of a lifetime of interests, passions, and memories. However, they must not be overlooked in the decluttering process.

Begin with books, which, for many, are not just reading material but treasured companions. Start by removing all the books from your shelves. Consider each one and ask yourself if it holds meaning for you or could be of value to someone else. It's important to be honest about whether each book will be reread or if it's time to pass it on. Consider donating books that no longer serve you to libraries, schools, or charity shops, where they can enrich the lives of others.

When it comes to media, such as DVDs, CDs, vinyl records, and even old cassettes or VHS tapes, reflect on the likelihood of revisiting these formats. With the digital age offering more compact and accessible ways to enjoy music and films, physical copies may be redundant. Digitize what you can't bear to part with, and find new homes for the rest. Some collectors and enthusiasts would cherish these items, and selling or donating them can give them a second life.

Artwork presents a unique challenge, as it often carries a strong emotional attachment and can be one of the more personal possessions one owns. Start by identifying the pieces you genuinely love and resonate with you or your family. If there are pieces that no longer speak to you, consider whether they might be appreciated by friends, family, or even local art schools. Remember, the aim is not to strip away all sentiment but to curate a meaningful and manageable collection.

By thoughtfully curating your collection of books, media, and artwork, you declutter your space and create a legacy of cherished memories that truly matter to you.

Clothing and Textiles

Clothing and textiles often hold a significant emotional value, as they are closely tied to personal identity and memories. However, they also represent a substantial volume of possessions that can burden those we leave behind if not thoughtfully curated.

Gather all clothing, linens, towels, and other textiles into one area. This allows you to assess what you own clearly. Handle each item individually, considering its usefulness, condition, and emotional significance. Ask yourself when you last wore or used it, and be honest about the likelihood of it being used in the future.

For clothing, start with items that are easiest to part with. This might include pieces that no longer fit, are out of style, or damaged beyond repair. Consider the practicality of the garment – for instance, heavy winter coats may not be necessary to keep if you live in a mild climate or have multiple similar items.

As you sort, create separate piles for different actions: one for items to keep, one for donations, one for recycling, and one for textiles that are too worn to be used by someone else and might serve better as rags or in textile recycling programs. Be mindful of the quality and condition of items intended for donation – charities often spend considerable resources disposing of items that cannot be used.

When it comes to sentimental pieces, such as a wedding dress or a hand-knitted sweater from a loved one, consider if someone in your circle would cherish it as much as you have. If not, think creatively about how to honor the memory it represents. A photograph of the item worn at a significant event, accompanied by a written memory, can preserve the sentiment without the physical object.

For linens and towels, apply the same criteria. Keep enough sets for your needs and a few for guests, but let go of excess. Remember, items in good condition can be a welcome donation to animal shelters or charitable organizations.

Throughout this process, take breaks when needed and allow yourself to reminisce about the passing of time that these items represent. Focus on lightening the load for your loved ones and ensuring that those you keep reflect a thoughtful and intentional life.

By the end of this exercise, you should have a more manageable collection of clothing and textiles that serve your current life and will not impose an undue burden on your loved ones in the future.

Papers, Documents, and Personal Records

As we delve into papers, documents, and personal records, we enter a territory often fraught with emotional weight and practical complexity. Often tucked away in drawers, cabinets, and boxes, these items can accumulate over a lifetime into a formidable collection. The Swedish death cleaning process encourages us to approach these personal archives with purpose and clarity, ensuring that what we leave behind is meaningful and manageable for those we love.

Begin by gathering all your documents in one place. This may seem daunting, but it is essential for taking stock of what you have. Once assembled, categorize your papers into three groups: essential, important, and dispensable.

Essential documents are those that are crucial for legal and personal identification purposes. These include birth certificates, marriage licenses, passports, wills, living wills, powers of attorney, and other legal documents necessary for settling your affairs. These should be kept in a secure but accessible location, and it is wise to inform a trusted person about where these documents can be found.

Important documents may not be critical for legal purposes but hold significant personal or financial value. This category includes property deeds, mortgage papers, vehicle titles, insurance policies, tax returns, and investment records. While these should also be kept secure, consider digitizing them to reduce physical clutter and ensure their preservation.

Dispensable documents are the most numerous and often challenging to sort through. These include old letters, greeting cards, photographs, receipts, manuals, and warranties. Reflect on the sentimental value of each item. Ask yourself if it brings you joy, will be meaningful to others, or serves a practical purpose. It may be time to let it go if it does not meet any of these criteria.

When it comes to personal letters and photographs, consider the feelings of others before discarding them. You might find that family members cherish certain items you consider trivial. Offer these to relatives or friends who may appreciate them. Shredding or recycling is often the most responsible way to dispose of papers that are no longer needed.

Take your time to consider the significance of each document, and do not rush the decision-making process. By systematically addressing the accumulation of papers, documents, and personal records, you are simplifying your own life and easing the burden on those who will one day sift through your memories and milestones.

Chapter Summary

- Heirlooms and sentimental items could be offered to family members, while unneeded items can be sold or donated.
- Dispose of unsalvageable furniture and more oversized items responsibly, considering recycling options for materials like wood or metal.
- Electronics and appliances should be evaluated for utility and condition, with working items donated and obsolete ones appropriately recycled.
- Books, media, and artwork require a balance of practicality and sentimentality, with meaningful items kept and others donated or sold.
- Clothing and textiles should be sorted, with excess and unworn items donated or recycled and sentimental pieces creatively preserved or passed on.
- Papers, documents, and personal records can be categorized as essential, important, or dispensable, with sensitive items securely stored or digitized.

4

CLEANING AS YOU GO

In the heart of Swedish death cleaning lies a principle that is as much about the present as it is about the future: the Clean Space Philosophy. This concept is a mindset, a way of living that simplifies the process of letting go and promotes a sense of tranquility in our daily lives.

The Clean Space Philosophy encourages you to approach cleaning not as a monumental task to be undertaken in the distant future but as a series of small, manageable actions integrated into everyday life. It is about creating and maintaining an environment that reflects the serenity we wish to leave behind. This philosophy is rooted in the understanding that our surroundings have the power to impact our well-being and that by curating our spaces thoughtfully, we can foster a sense of peace and order.

To embody this philosophy, we must first accept that every object in our possession carries emotional, physical, or psychological weight. By acknowledging this, we can assess our belongings more discerningly, asking ourselves whether each item serves a purpose or brings joy. If it does neither, it may be time to part with it. This is not to say that everything must go; it is about recognizing and holding onto what truly matters.

As we progress through our decluttering journey, it is essential to do so with intention. Each item we choose to keep should have a designated place within our home, a space where it belongs and contributes to the overall harmony of the environment. This deliberate placement of objects makes it easier to find what we need when we need it and creates a sense of order that is visually calming and mentally soothing.

The Clean Space Philosophy is about regular reflection and reassessment. As our lives evolve, so do our needs and preferences. What was once essential may no longer serve us, and what once brought happiness may no longer resonate. By periodically reviewing our possessions, we can ensure that our spaces remain aligned with our current selves rather than becoming time capsules of who we once were.

This philosophy is about cultivating a living environment that mirrors the clarity we seek in life. It is about recognizing that each day offers an opportunity to make choices that bring us closer to the essence of who we are and the legacy we wish to leave. By cleaning as we go, we not only ease the burden on ourselves and our loved ones in the future, but we also enhance the quality of our daily existence, creating a sanctuary that supports and reflects our journey through life.

Maintaining Order During the Process

As we progress further in our Swedish death cleaning journey, it is essential to recognize that the process is not simply a one-time event but a continuous practice of maintaining order. The philosophy of cleaning as you go is about instilling a sense of harmony and tranquility in your living space.

To maintain order during the process, remember to approach each task with mindfulness and intention. Set realistic goals for each cleaning session. Whether it's a single drawer, a closet, or a room, focus on that area and resist the urge to jump from one task to another. This targeted approach prevents feeling overwhelmed and keeps the process manageable.

As you sort through your belongings, categorize them into distinct piles or boxes and deal with each category promptly to avoid accumulating items that can lead to disorder over time. Assign the items you keep to a specific place in your home. This helps locate them when needed and discourages the piling up of unnecessary objects in the future. If you find items belonging to other family members or friends, set them aside so you can discuss their fate together. Swedish death cleaning is, after all, a considerate and communicative process.

During the cleaning sessions, take the time to clean the spaces that have been cleared. Wipe down shelves, vacuum or sweep the floors, and ensure that each item you return to its place is clean and in good condition. This habit contributes to the overall cleanliness of your home and the preservation of your belongings.

Be patient with yourself. Maintaining order is not about perfection; it's about progress. There will be days when you feel you've accomplished a lot and others when it seems you've barely made a dent. Acknowledge the effort you've put in and the steps you've taken towards a less cluttered and more intentional living space.

Lastly, remember to reflect on the emotional journey accompanying the physical act of cleaning. With each object you let go of, you're also releasing memories and attachments. Allow yourself to feel these emotions, reminisce, and come to terms with the impermanence of material possessions. This reflective process is integral to Swedish death cleaning, as it cleanses your home and provides clarity and peace of mind.

By maintaining order using these helpful pieces of advice, you are preparing for the eventualities of life and creating a serene environment that enhances your daily living. Swedish death cleaning can be an enriching and life-affirming process when done methodically and with intention.

Eco-Friendly Cleaning Practices

Another aspect to consider during the process is the environmental impact of our cleaning practices. The ethos of döstädning is also about minimizing our ecological footprint. In this spirit, let's explore eco-friendly cleaning practices that align with the thoughtful and purposeful approach of Swedish death cleaning.

Firstly, recognize the power of simplicity in cleaning agents. Commercial cleaning products often contain chemicals that can harm our health and the environment. Instead, consider natural alternatives like white vinegar, baking soda, and lemon juice, which are effective, non-toxic, and biodegradable. These simple ingredients can tackle various cleaning tasks, from descaling a kettle to freshening up laundry.

Use reusable cloths and sponges rather than disposable paper towels when scrubbing and wiping surfaces. Microfiber cloths, for instance, are highly absorbent and can be washed and reused countless times, reducing waste. If you prefer something more natural, consider bamboo or organic cotton cloths.

In decluttering, you might come across old t-shirts or towels. Rather than discarding them, repurpose them into cleaning rags. This extends the life of these materials and reduces the need to purchase new cleaning cloths.

For those items that require a deeper clean, such as carpets or upholstered furniture, look for eco-friendly professional services that use non-toxic cleaning methods. Alternatively, renting or investing in a steam cleaner for personal use can be a chemical-free way to refresh these items without the environmental toll of conventional cleaning solutions.

Consider the most environmentally responsible methods when disposing of items that no longer serve a purpose in your life. Recycle what you can, donate items still in good condition, and responsibly discard electronics and hazardous materials according to local regulations.

Lastly, remember that the goal is not only to leave behind a tidy and considerate legacy but also to do so in a way that honors the environment. By integrating eco-friendly cleaning practices into this process, you contribute to a healthier planet for current and future generations.

Dealing with Dust, Dirt, and Grime

The Swedish death cleaning philosophy extends beyond merely sorting and discarding items. It encompasses the meticulous care of our living spaces, ensuring they remain clean, orderly, and pleasant. As we adopt the principles of 'döstädning,' we should also focus on the persistent adversaries of cleanliness: dust, dirt, and grime.

These elements are reminders of the passage of time and the accumulation of life's residues. Addressing them is not a sporadic battle but a continuous process. It is about maintaining an environment that reflects our respect for our possessions and the eventual ease of transition for those we leave behind.

To deal with dust, begin with the high surfaces and work your way down. Use a microfiber cloth or a duster with an extendable handle to reach the tops of bookshelves, picture frames, and light fixtures. This method ensures that any dislodged particles will ultimately find their way to the floor, where they can be swept or vacuumed away in the final cleaning stages.

When confronting dirt and grime, especially in high-traffic areas or places where spills and stains are common, acting swiftly and with the appropriate cleaning agents is essential. For hard surfaces, a mixture of warm water and mild dish soap can be effective, while a baking soda paste might be necessary for more stubborn grime. Always test a small, inconspicuous area first to ensure the cleaning solution does not damage the surface.

In the case of upholstery and fabrics, vacuuming regularly is crucial to prevent the embedding of dirt and dust. For stains, use a cleaner suitable for the fabric type and blot gently, avoiding harsh scrubbing that can damage the fibers.

Throughout this process, take a moment to reflect on the items you are cleaning. Each object has a story and a connection to your life. As you wipe away the dust and grime, you are also reaffirming your decisions about what to keep and what to let go. This cleaning becomes a physical manifestation of our internal contemplation, an organized practice that cleans our homes and clears our minds.

Integrating these cleaning practices into our routine ensures that our living spaces remain decluttered and reflect a well-loved life. It is a gift of consideration to ourselves and those who will one day be responsible for our cherished belongings. Maintaining cleanliness is an act of kindness that will echo into the future.

Final Touches for a Refreshed Space

Having addressed the removal of dust, dirt, and grime, we can now turn our attention to the final touches that transform a clean space into a refreshed and harmonious environment. This step is as much about cleanliness as it is about creating a sense of peace and harmony that can be felt by anyone who enters the space.

Begin by stepping back and surveying the room. After thoroughly cleaning, the space should already feel more open and inviting. However, the final touches are about fine-tuning the area to ensure it feels truly finished and welcoming. This involves a few key steps that are often overlooked but essential for achieving the desired effect.

Firstly, consider the placement of furniture and objects. During the cleaning process, items may have been moved around to allow for a more thorough job. Now is the time to thoughtfully rearrange these pieces to optimize the flow and functionality of the room. In the spirit of döstädning, this may also be an opportunity to reassess the necessity of certain items. If something no longer serves a purpose or brings joy, it may be time to let it go.

Next, focus on the more minor details. Polish mirrors and glass surfaces to a streak-free shine, as these can often show the remnants of cleaning products if not properly attended to. Fluff cushions and straighten throws to give a lived-in yet tidy appearance to seating areas. These small actions contribute significantly to the overall sense of order and comfort.

Lighting plays a pivotal role in the ambiance of a room. Adjust the window treatments to allow natural light to filter in, enhancing the freshness of the space. If the room is used in the evening, ensure the lighting is warm and inviting. A well-placed lamp or a dimmer switch can make all the difference in creating a cozy atmosphere.

Finally, add a personal touch that signifies the completion of the cleaning process. This could be a fresh bouquet of flowers placed in a vase, a scented candle, or a piece of art with special meaning. These elements serve as a reminder of the care and intention put into the cleaning process and the importance of maintaining a space that reflects the best aspects of one's life.

These final touches are about more than just aesthetics; they reaffirm the values and memories we wish to preserve and pass on. By methodically and reflectively approaching this last stage, we not only create a space that is clean and organized but also one that will bring joy to our everyday lives.

Chapter Summary

- The Clean Space Philosophy emphasizes living with tranquility by integrating small cleaning actions into daily life.
- Regular reflection and reassessment of belongings are encouraged to align living spaces with current needs and preferences.
- Maintaining order during cleaning involves setting realistic goals, categorizing items, and cleaning spaces as they are cleared.
- Eco-friendly cleaning practices are recommended, such as using natural cleaning agents and repurposing old materials for cleaning rags.
- Dust, dirt, and grime should be addressed methodically, with appropriate cleaning agents and techniques for different surfaces.

- Final touches in the cleaning process involve thoughtful placement of furniture, polishing surfaces, optimizing lighting, and adding personal touches.
- Swedish death cleaning is a continuous process that not only prepares for the future but also creates a serene environment for the present.

5

MEMORIES AND MEMENTOS

As we find ourselves sifting through the tangible remnants of our lives—photographs, letters, and keepsakes— each item can evoke a spectrum of emotions, from joy to sorrow, nostalgia to resolve. In curating your life story through these mementos, you are not only reflecting on the past but also shaping the legacy you wish to leave behind.

Selecting which memories to preserve and which to let go of is akin to editing a manuscript of your life. It requires a discerning eye and a thoughtful heart. Here is some guidance to help you sort through these possessions carefully and intentionally.

Begin by gathering all your mementos in one place, creating a physical timeline of your life. As you examine each item, ask yourself: Does this object still hold meaning? Is it tied to a person or an event significant to me or my loved ones? Will it bring joy or comfort to those I leave behind?

It is important to recognize that not all possessions are created equal in emotional value. Some items may be intrinsically linked to pivotal moments or relationships. In contrast, others, upon reflection, may be mere placeholders for memories that reside securely in your mind. It is the former that merit a place in your curated collection.

As you make these decisions, consider the stories these objects tell. A well-worn recipe card, annotated with notes and stains, tells a tale of family gatherings and shared meals. A collection of postcards may map out a lifetime of travels and adventures. These items are all part of your life story, a narrative you will pass on.

In this process, it is also essential to be mindful of the quantity of items you choose to keep. A life story distilled into a few cherished possessions can often speak louder than a volume of cluttered memories. This is not to say that you should strip your history to the bare bones, but rather to select those pieces that best represent the essence of your journey.

Remember, too, that this curation is not a solitary task. Engage with family and friends, sharing the stories behind your treasures. Their insights may help you see the value in items you overlooked, or they may lovingly relieve you of the burden of objects that hold more meaning for them than for you.

Ultimately, the goal of curating your life story is not to create a shrine to oneself but to craft a thoughtful collection that honors your past, brings peace in the present, and will be cherished by those who continue your story into the future.

Creating Keepsakes and Legacy Boxes

As we sift through our personal treasures, we may wonder how best to preserve these stories for future generations. This is where the concept of creating keepsakes and legacy boxes comes into play.

A keepsake is an item that holds personal value and evokes memories of a particular time, person, or event. It is something to be cherished and passed down through the family as a token of remembrance. On the other hand, a legacy box is a carefully curated collection of such keepsakes thoughtfully assembled to convey a narrative of one's life journey.

You may wish to create a legacy box for some of your most sentimental items. Selecting items for a legacy box requires a reflective and systematic approach. Begin by choosing a container that feels appropriate for the treasures it will hold. This could be a beautifully crafted wooden box, a sturdy archival storage box, or even a simple yet elegant cardboard box. The container itself can be a part of the legacy, reflecting the aesthetic preferences of its assembler.

As you decide on the contents, consider the stories each item tells. A legacy box is more than just a repository for things; it is a vessel for stories, a way to communicate values, experiences, and the essence of who you are. Include items that have a narrative quality: letters, photographs, a cherished book, or a piece of jewelry that has been passed down through generations. Each of these items should serve as a chapter in the story of your life.

You could include a personal note or a descriptive label with each item. This narrative can explain the significance of the object, the context in which it was received or used, and why it has been chosen to be part of the legacy. These descriptions will provide clarity and meaning for those who will one day sift through these memories.

Balancing emotional value with practical considerations is vital when creating keepsakes and legacy boxes. Be selective and avoid overfilling the box. The goal is to distill a life's worth of memories into a collection that is meaningful, manageable, and, most importantly, reflective of yourself.

As you curate these items, you may find yourself reminiscing and reflecting on the life you've led. This process is about leaving a legacy for others and reviewing and appreciating the life you have lived. It is a chance to acknowledge your journey, the people who have been part of it, and the moments that have defined you.

Creating keepsakes and legacy boxes is an act of love, a final gift to your loved ones, and a way to ensure that your story is told and remembered.

Digital Memories and Online Presence

In the modern age, the concept of mementos extends beyond the tangible. As we continue our journey of reflection and self-discovery, we must also consider the digital footprint we leave behind. Digital memories and online presence form a significant part of our legacy, and managing them can be as meaningful as handling physical belongings.

Our digital lives are composed of photographs, videos, social media profiles, blogs, and email accounts, each holding pieces of our narratives. These virtual keepsakes are often overlooked during the decluttering process. Yet, they require our attention to ensure that our digital legacy aligns with our wishes and provides a clear, curated story, free from clutter for those we leave behind.

Begin by taking inventory of your digital assets. List all the platforms and accounts where you have a presence. This includes social media profiles, cloud storage services, email accounts, and any websites or blogs you own. Reflect on what each of these digital spaces represents about you and how they contribute to the story you wish to tell.

For social media accounts, consider downloading a copy of your data, which is often a feature offered by the platforms. This lets you keep a personal archive of your interactions, photos, and posts. Once you have this archive, you might deactivate certain profiles or leave instructions on handling them when you are no longer around. Some platforms have legacy contact options, enabling a trusted person to manage your account after you pass away.

Photographs and videos stored in the cloud or digital devices are precious memories that can be shared with loved ones. Organize these by creating folders for different periods or events and label them clearly. You might also consider transferring these to a dedicated external hard drive or creating shared online albums for family and friends to access.

Email accounts often contain a mix of important documents and casual correspondence. Sift through your emails, deleting what is no longer necessary and organizing the rest into folders. It's also wise to leave instructions on handling your email accounts, including login information, as part of your digital estate planning.

For blogs and personal websites, decide if you want them to remain online as a record of your interests and thoughts. If so, ensure that the hosting fees are taken care of and that someone knows how to manage the content in your absence.

By taking these steps, you ensure that your digital memories and online presence are preserved and presented in a way that honors your life story. Just as with physical items, the goal is to leave behind a digital space that is organized, meaningful, and reflective of your life. This thoughtful approach to your digital legacy is a gift to those who will cherish your memory long after you're gone.

Sharing Stories with Family

Sharing stories with family is a crucial step in this journey. It breathes life into cherished objects and ensures their legacy continues even as we consider letting them go. This stage of the process is less about the physical act of decluttering and more about the emotional resonance of the items we hold dear.

When we engage with our family members in the storytelling of our possessions, we do more than recount the past; we create a bridge to the future. Each item, from a simple handwritten letter to a well-worn piece of jewelry, carries a narrative that, when shared, can offer comfort, instill values, and even impart wisdom. Through these shared narratives, our belongings transcend their material form and become part of our family's collective memory.

When you undertake this process, you might want to gather your family in a comfortable setting, free from the distractions of daily life. Approach the conversation with a sense of openness and invite your loved ones to ask questions. As you pick up each memento, allow yourself to delve into the memories it conjures. Describe the context in which the item was received or purchased, the people associated with it, and the reasons it has been significant in your life.

It is important to be reflective and honest during these exchanges. Some stories may evoke laughter, while others might summon tears. Both reactions are valuable and contribute to the richness of your history. Encourage family members to share their recollections and associations with the items. This can be particularly enlightening, as the same object may hold different meanings for different people.

As you share these stories, consider the practical aspects of Swedish death cleaning. Discuss with your family who might like to inherit certain items. This is an opportunity to match possessions with those who will truly appreciate and honor their history. It is also a chance to let go of things that, while once meaningful, no longer serve a purpose or bring joy.

Sometimes, while the physical item is not needed, the story behind it is precious. In these instances, documenting the narrative can be a powerful alternative to keeping the object. Write down the tales or record them, creating a lasting record that can be revisited and cherished for future generations.

Sharing stories with family is part of an ongoing conversation. It is a process that can be revisited as you continue to sort through your belongings and as your family's dynamics evolve. Doing this ensures that the essence of your memories is preserved, even if you make the thoughtful decision to part with the physical mementos.

Preserving Important Family History

Döstädning allows us to confront the tangible fragments of our past —those objects that carry the weight of our personal and family history. As we sift through the layers of belongings, we often unearth mementos that are more than mere objects; they are the keepers of stories, the physical manifestations of our lineage and legacy. Preserving these important pieces of family history is both a gift to our descendants and a way to honor the lives that have preceded our own.

The process begins with discernment. Certain pieces stand out as irreplaceable conduits to the past among the myriad of items that fill our homes. These may include photographs, handwritten letters, diaries, military medals, or even a simple recipe card in a loved one's handwriting. Each of these items holds a thread that, when woven together, creates the rich narrative of a family's history.

To preserve these treasures, we must first ensure their physical longevity. This involves practical measures such as storing paper items in acid-free sleeves, keeping photographs out of direct sunlight, and protecting delicate textiles from the ravages of time and environment. It is also advisable to digitize these items, creating electronic copies that can be shared and saved without physical deterioration.

But preservation goes beyond mere conservation of the object; it involves safeguarding the stories they represent. Take the time to document the history behind each memento. Who did this belong to? What is the story of its significance? Recording these details can be as simple as writing a note to accompany the item or as elaborate as creating a digital archive with narratives, images, and scanned documents.

Sharing these preserved items with family members can be a deeply meaningful experience. It provides an opportunity to connect with relatives over shared heritage and to pass on the stories of ancestors to younger generations. Consider creating a family history box or scrapbook that can be added to over time and passed down through the generations.

In the spirit of döstädning, it is vital to be selective. Not every item needs to be kept for posterity. Choose those that truly encapsulate the essence of your family's story and let go of the rest with gratitude for their role in your journey. This selective process not only eases the burden on those who will one day sift through our possessions but also highlights the most significant chapters of our family narrative.

Preserving important family history is a balancing act between honoring the past and embracing the impermanence of life. It is a thoughtful process that allows us to curate a legacy, ensuring that the stories and memories that shape us are not lost to time but are held close, ready to be retold and cherished by the generations to come.

Chapter Summary

- Sorting through tangible mementos like photos and letters is like editing a life story, requiring a discerning eye to choose items with emotional value and significance to oneself and loved ones.
- Not all possessions hold the same emotional value; it's essential to curate a collection that truly represents one's life journey.
- Creating keepsakes and legacy boxes involves selecting meaningful items that tell the story of one's life to be cherished by future generations.
- Engaging family and friends in the process can provide different perspectives and help determine the significance of items.
- Digital memories, such as social media profiles and online photos, are also part of one's legacy and should be curated with care and intention.
- Sharing stories with family about cherished items can create a bridge to the future and ensure the legacy of these objects continues.
- Preserving important family history involves being selective with items, ensuring their physical and narrative preservation, and sharing them with family.

6

THE EMOTIONAL JOURNEY

Throughout the process, you must be prepared for the emotional ebbs and flows that accompany the sorting and letting go of a lifetime's accumulation of belongings. It is a unique and personal journey that often brings to the surface various memories and feelings intertwined with the objects we have cherished.

As you navigate through the highs and lows of this journey, acknowledge that each item you touch may evoke a spectrum of emotions. The highs can be moments of rediscovery and joy as you unearth forgotten photographs that bring back the laughter of a summer long past or a treasured gift from a dear friend that reminds you of a bond that time or distance could erode. These moments buoy your spirits and remind you of the love and experiences that have colored your life.

Conversely, the lows can manifest as a sense of loss or grief. Parting with items can feel like saying goodbye to a part of yourself, a tangible connection to your past that you are not yet ready to sever. It may be a piece of furniture that has been the silent witness to your family's history or a collection of letters that speak of a younger self with dreams and aspirations now transformed by time.

Letting go can sometimes feel like you're erasing these chapters of your life. Approach these emotional lows with compassion and patience. Allow yourself to feel the weight of these emotions, to sit with the sadness or the longing that may arise. It is a natural response to the closing of a chapter, an integral part of acknowledging and honoring your life's journey.

There is also an opportunity for growth and self-reflection in this emotional landscape. With each decision to keep or part with an item, you reaffirm your values and priorities. You are distilling the essence of your life story, deciding what is truly significant and what can be released. This discernment is empowering, as it clarifies what you wish to leave behind as your legacy.

Remember, Swedish death cleaning is not just about the physical act of decluttering but also about the emotional reckoning with one's mortality and the impermanence of life. It is a chance to confront the reality that we will all be a memory one day. In this confrontation, a great opportunity exists to shape that memory with intention and thoughtfulness.

As you continue on this journey, take solace in the knowledge that the emotional highs and lows reflect a life fully lived, the connections you've made, and the impact you've had on the world around you. Embrace the process as a meaningful ritual, an act of caring for those you will one day leave behind.

Attachment and Identity

Throughout the cleaning process, we confront the physical accumulation of a lifetime and the intricate web of attachment and identity that our possessions represent. This practice, while pragmatic in its approach to decluttering, is deeply interwoven with the emotional fabric of our being. It is a poignant reminder that the items we gather are more than mere objects; they are the silent narrators of our personal history, the tangible touchstones of our identity.

As we sift through the layers of belongings, we often stumble upon items that are heavy with memory and meaning. A simple piece of jewelry may carry the weight of a thousand moments, a book may open to a page that once offered solace, and a photograph may freeze time in a frame, holding faces and places that have long since changed. These are the artifacts of our existence, the physical manifestations of our joys, sorrows, achievements, and relationships.

Therefore, the act of letting go becomes more than a practical tidying up; it is a reflective journey through the chapters of one's life. Each decision to keep or discard an item is a negotiation with the past, a dialogue between the person we once were and the one we have become. It requires us to ask ourselves difficult questions about what is truly important and what legacy we wish to leave behind.

In this delicate dance of detachment, we may find that our sense of self is not diminished but rather distilled. By releasing the physical anchors of our past, we grant ourselves the freedom to redefine our identity. We learn that while objects can signify love, achievement, or heritage, they do not encapsulate the entirety of our existence. Our worth is not measured by the things we own but by the experiences we've had, the relationships we've nurtured, and the growth we've fostered within ourselves.

Swedish death cleaning, then, is as much an inward journey as it is a physical undertaking. It is an opportunity to reassess and reaffirm our values, acknowledge the impermanence of material possessions, and embrace the essence of who we are beyond the clutter. As we prepare our belongings for their eventual parting from us, we are also preparing ourselves for a future unburdened by the unnecessary. In this future, our identity is not tied to the objects we leave behind but to the memories and love we've shared.

Coping with Loss and Grief

As we sift through our belongings, we are inevitably faced with the memories and sentiments attached to them, and this can lead us into the depths of loss and grief. It is a natural part of the journey, requiring both acknowledgment and navigation with care.

Loss and grief are not solely the domain of those who have passed. They are also experienced by the living, who must grapple with the void left behind. In the context of death cleaning, these emotions can surface as we handle items that once belonged to loved ones or as we contemplate our mortality and the legacy we wish to leave.

Sorting personal belongings can trigger grief, as each item might evoke a memory, moment, or shared experience. It is not uncommon to feel a wave of sadness when holding a garment that still carries the scent of a departed loved one or when stumbling upon a handwritten note that speaks from the past. These tangible pieces of history serve as conduits to our emotions, and it is essential to honor these feelings rather than suppress them.

To cope with the grief that may arise during death cleaning, it is helpful to approach the task with a sense of ritual and respect. Allow yourself moments of reflection when they are needed. It is okay to pause, remember, and feel the full weight of what these objects represent. Some may find solace in sharing stories about the items with family or friends. In contrast, others may prefer to sit in quiet contemplation.

Recognize that grief does not always follow a linear path. There may be days when the burden seems lighter, and sorting through belongings feels like a celebration of life rather than a reminder of loss. On other days, the sorrow may feel overwhelming. Be patient with yourself and understand that this is a normal part of the emotional journey.

While coping with loss and grief, there is also an opportunity for growth and understanding. By letting go, we can come to terms with our past, reconcile with our present, and make peace with the inevitability of change. Though fraught with emotional challenges, this journey can ultimately lead to a place of acceptance and serenity.

In our lives, it is essential to find balance. Allow grief its time, but also seek out the moments of lightness and joy that can emerge from releasing the old and making space for new experiences. In the next section, we will explore how the act of letting go can be not only a process of decluttering but also a gratifying act of self-discovery and renewal.

Finding Joy in Letting Go

Letting go is a release of the past, clearing space for the future. This journey can lead to unexpected joy and a deep sense of liberation.

As we sift through the layers of belongings, we often stumble upon items that have been long forgotten, tucked away in the corners of drawers or the back of closets. These rediscovered treasures can evoke a complex array of memories, some tinged with nostalgia, others with regret. It is natural to feel a reluctance to part with these objects, as they seem to be tangible links to the experiences and people that have shaped us.

However, a subtle but powerful joy emerges when we give ourselves permission to let go. When we engage in the act of discarding or donating, we not only gain satisfaction, but also recognise that in doing so, we are honoring our past while making room for new experiences. We are not erasing memories but acknowledging that they exist within us, independent of the physical objects that may trigger them.

The joy in letting go also comes from the understanding that our possessions can have a second life that extends beyond our own. By passing on items to family, friends, or even strangers, we allow our belongings to serve a new purpose, to bring happiness or utility to others. This generosity can be incredibly fulfilling, as it connects us to a larger community and contributes to a cycle of giving that has meaningful implications.

The process of letting go can be an opportunity for self-discovery. As we evaluate what to keep and what to release, we are prompted to reflect on what truly matters to us. This introspection can lead to a clearer sense of our values and priorities and influence how we live our lives moving forward. The space we create by decluttering can be both literal and figurative, allowing us to breathe more freely and focus on the aspects of life that bring us the most joy.

In embracing the concept of finding joy in letting go, we also embrace a form of mindfulness. It is a practice that requires us to be present in the moment, engage with our emotions, and make conscious decisions about what we choose to surround ourselves with. This mindfulness can extend to other areas of our lives, encouraging us to live more intentionally and to appreciate the present.

The emotional journey of Swedish death cleaning is not without its challenges. Still, it is a path that can lead to a lighter, more joyful existence. As we learn to let go, we open ourselves up to new possibilities and affirm that our happiness is not bound by the material world but a reflection of the love, relationships, and experiences that truly define us.

The Role of Reflection and Mindfulness

Throughout the pages of this book, we have come to understand that decluttering is far more than a mere physical task; it is a profoundly emotional and reflective journey. As we sift through the layers of our material possessions, we are also sifting through the layers of our lives, memories, and the very essence of our being. This is where the role of reflection and mindfulness becomes paramount.

Reflection, in the context of Swedish death cleaning, is the deliberate act of contemplating the significance of each item in our possession. It is about asking ourselves why we have held onto particular objects and whether they continue to serve a purpose in our lives or those we will one day leave behind. This introspective approach allows us to make decisions not out of haste or obligation but from a place of conscious choice.

On the other hand, mindfulness is the practice of being fully present in the moment and aware of our thoughts and feelings without judgment. As we engage in decluttering, mindfulness keeps us centered and grounded. It helps us to recognize the emotional responses that arise—be it joy, sadness, or nostalgia—and to honor those feelings without becoming overwhelmed by them.

Reflection and mindfulness create a space for us to engage with our belongings thoughtfully and intentionally. By being reflective, we permit ourselves to acknowledge the past, the memories associated with our possessions, and their roles in our lives. By being mindful, we stay connected to the present, ensuring that our actions align with our current values and the legacy we wish to leave.

This process is an opportunity to reassess what we truly value, simplify our lives, and make peace with the impermanence of all things. In embracing reflection and mindfulness, we not only prepare our homes for a future without us, but we also cultivate a sense of peace and fulfillment in the here and now, knowing that we are living—and leaving—a life that is both intentional and meaningful.

Chapter Summary

- Swedish death cleaning involves emotional challenges as one sorts through a lifetime of possessions, evoking memories and feelings.
- The practice is not just about decluttering but also about confronting mortality and the impermanence of life.
- The process can bring joy from rediscovering cherished items but also sadness from parting with objects tied to one's identity.
- Letting go of items can feel like an erasure of life chapters, requiring compassion and patience to handle the emotional lows.
- Deciding what to keep or discard is empowering, helping to reaffirm values and shape one's legacy. It's a reflective journey, prompting questions about the importance of possessions and their role in defining identity.
- Coping with loss and grief is part of the process, with some days feeling lighter and others more sorrowful.
- Finding joy in letting go can lead to liberation, self-discovery, and a more intentional life, unburdened by unnecessary items.

7

PRACTICAL MATTERS

In this section of the book, we will focus on how to handle legal documents and financial affairs. This is a cornerstone of ensuring that our affairs are in order, both for our peace of mind and to ease the burden on those we leave behind.

Begin with gathering all relevant legal documents. These may include wills, trusts, deeds, and titles. It is essential to keep these documents up to date and in a secure yet accessible location.

Inform a trusted family member or friend about where these documents can be found. If you have appointed an executor for your estate, ensure that this individual knows their responsibilities and the location of these critical documents.

Next, consider your financial affairs. Compile a comprehensive list of bank accounts, investments, insurance policies, and outstanding debts. This list should include institution names, account numbers, and contact information for each entity. It is also wise to include a summary of your regular bills and subscriptions, as these will need to be managed or canceled accordingly.

Reflect on the importance of transparency in these matters. It is not uncommon to feel a sense of privacy about one's finances. However, in the context of death cleaning, openness can prevent unnecessary complications during an already challenging time. Consider writing a letter of instruction that goes beyond the legal formality of a will. This letter can guide your loved ones on how you wish your affairs to be handled and can include personal sentiments and explanations that legal documents may not convey.

As you organize these elements, consider any safe deposit boxes, storage units, and physical items of significant monetary or sentimental value. Document these and communicate their existence and your intentions for them.

In this process, it is advisable to consult with a legal professional to ensure that all documents are in order and that your wishes are articulated and legally sound. This step can prevent disputes and confusion, allowing your loved ones to focus on honoring your memory rather than deciphering legal complexities.

As we conclude this section on legal documents and financial affairs, we pave the way for the next step in Swedish death cleaning: addressing digital assets and passwords. In our modern age, these elements have become integral to our daily lives and, consequently, to the legacy we leave behind.

Addressing Digital Assets and Passwords

Our lives are increasingly intertwined with the digital world in the modern era. As we consider the practical matters of decluttering and organizing our lives, we must pay due attention to our digital assets and passwords. This aspect of death cleaning is about ensuring that our digital legacy is handled with the same care and respect as our physical possessions. We discussed the handling of digital memories in earlier chapters, but this section will explore digital assets in more detail.

Digital assets encompass various elements, from social media accounts and email to online banking and investment portfolios. They also include personal items such as digital photos, videos, and documents often stored in cloud services or various devices. Managing these assets is a two-fold process: first, identifying them, and second, ensuring that loved ones can access them when the time comes.

Begin by creating a comprehensive inventory of your digital assets. This list should include all online accounts and the corresponding usernames and passwords. It's important to keep this inventory updated and to store it securely. Several methods exist to manage this sensitive information, including password managers, encrypted digital storage, or a physical document kept in a safe or with a trusted individual.

Consider how you would like each account handled when documenting your digital assets. Some platforms have policies in place for the accounts of deceased users, and you may have the option to select a legacy contact or set up an account to be memorialized. For other accounts, you may wish to provide instructions on whether they should be deleted, archived, or transferred to someone else.

It's also crucial to understand the legal implications of transferring digital assets. Laws regarding digital property after death may evolve, and it's wise to consult with an attorney to ensure that your wishes are enforceable and that you're adhering to the terms of service agreements for each platform.

Lastly, consider the security of your digital assets. Securely store your passwords, access codes, and any other necessary information so that a trusted individual can access them when the time comes. Digital legacy services and password managers are designed for this purpose, which can simplify the process for your loved ones.

Remember to review and address your digital assets periodically. As technology changes and new platforms emerge, revisit your inventory regularly to add new accounts and remove those no longer active. Communicate with your loved ones about your digital estate plan so they know your wishes and where to find the necessary information when needed.

Incorporating digital assets into your Swedish death cleaning process is a thoughtful way to ease the burden on your loved ones and protect your digital legacy. By taking these methodical steps, you can ensure that your online presence is managed with the same dignity and intention as the rest of your estate.

Estate Planning and Wills

Estate planning and drafting wills are critical components of the death cleaning process, ensuring that our material possessions and assets are distributed according to our wishes upon our departure from this world.

Estate planning is not just a task for older people or the wealthy; it is a practical step for anyone who wishes to have a say in handling their affairs after they are gone. It involves a clear and legally binding document, typically known as a will, which outlines the distribution of one's assets and the care of any dependents. This document serves as a voice that speaks on your behalf, providing instructions and decisions that must be respected and followed.

When engaging in estate planning, it is wise to begin by taking a comprehensive inventory of your assets. These include real estate, bank accounts, investments, insurance policies, and personal items of value such as jewelry, art, or heirlooms. Once the inventory is complete, consider the beneficiaries who will receive parts of your estate. They could be family members, friends, or charitable organizations you wish to support.

Selecting an executor, a trusted individual responsible for carrying out the instructions in your will, is also crucial. This role requires a person who is both willing and able to handle the legal and financial responsibilities that come with the distribution of an estate. It is a role of great trust and should be considered carefully.

In addition to the distribution of assets, a will can include the designation of guardians for minor children, instructions for the continuation or dissolution of a business, and even the care of pets. These personal preferences make your will a unique and personal document, reflecting your assets, values, and wishes.

While the process may seem daunting, numerous resources are available to assist in estate planning. Legal professionals specializing in wills and estates can provide invaluable guidance, ensuring that your will is comprehensive and compliant with current laws. There are also do-it-yourself kits and software for those with straightforward estates. However, professional advice is always recommended to avoid oversights or legal complications.

Once your will is drafted, it is not a document to be tucked away and forgotten. Life's circumstances change, and so too should your will. Regular reviews and updates are necessary to ensure that it accurately reflects your wishes. Major life events such as marriage, divorce, the birth of a child, or the acquisition of significant assets are all reasons to revisit your will.

In the spirit of Swedish death cleaning, estate planning and wills are not about dwelling on the end of life but rather about ensuring peace of mind for yourself and your loved ones. It is an act of kindness and consideration, a way to ease the burden on those who remain and to leave an orderly and transparent legacy.

We will now shift our focus from the tangible aspects of our estate to the more personal and intimate considerations of our final wishes. This naturally leads us to contemplate our funeral wishes and advanced directives, which will be explored in the following section.

Funeral Wishes and Advanced Directives

In the process of Swedish death cleaning, there is a component that often goes unaddressed until it is too late: the articulation of funeral wishes and the creation of advanced directives. You don't have to wait until the later years of your life to consider these aspects. This section will guide you through the thoughtful process of making and documenting these crucial decisions properly.

Funeral wishes can vary widely from individual to individual. Some may desire a traditional burial, while others prefer cremation followed by a memorial service. Some wish for their remains to be scattered in a place of significance, and others opt for newer methods, such as green burials. The key is to reflect on what would be most meaningful to you and your family and to make these wishes known.

Begin by contemplating the type of service you would like. Consider the music, readings, or any specific rituals that hold personal significance. Think about who you would want to speak or perform at the service. These details can offer comfort and a sense of closeness to your loved ones as they carry out your final wishes.

Once you have a clear idea of your preferences, it is crucial to document them. A written plan can be kept with your important papers, such as your will or estate plan, and should be accessible to your next of kin or executor. While this document does not carry the legal weight of a will, it serves as a guide to your loved ones and helps to ensure your wishes are respected.

Advanced directives, on the other hand, are legally binding documents that outline your medical care preferences if you cannot communicate them yourself. These include living wills and health care proxies or durable powers of attorney for health care. A living will details the types of medical treatments you would or would not want to receive in various scenarios, while a health care proxy appoints someone to make medical decisions on your behalf.

Discussing your thoughts and decisions with the person you intend to name as your healthcare proxy is advisable. This conversation can be challenging, but they must understand your values and desires regarding end-of-life care. Additionally, ensure that your healthcare providers have copies of these documents and that they are included in your medical records.

By taking the time to address these matters, you gain peace of mind and provide clarity and direction to those managing your affairs. This foresight is a final act of kindness that relieves your loved ones of the burden of guesswork during a time of grief.

Addressing funeral wishes and advanced directives is a continuation of the thoughtful consideration for the well-being of those we leave behind. It is a way to maintain control over our final narrative and impart a sense of order and calm when needed.

Communicating Your Plans Clearly

Clear communication is important throughout this process. It is a task that requires introspection and the ability to convey your intentions and decisions to those affected by them. After addressing the sensitive topics of funeral wishes and advanced directives, it is essential to pivot towards the broader scope of your plans and how to share them effectively.

To begin, consider creating a comprehensive document that outlines the specifics of your death cleaning process. This document should guide your loved ones, detailing what you have done, why you have made certain choices, and where important items are located. Transparency is vital; the more your family understands your rationale, the easier it will be for them to respect and carry out your wishes.

When communicating your plans, it's essential to be as detailed as possible. For instance, if you have earmarked particular possessions for specific individuals, make a list that matches items with their intended recipients. This will help to prevent misunderstandings and disputes among family members when you are no longer around. If you have decided to donate specific items to charity or sell them, provide instructions on how this should be done, perhaps even suggesting specific organizations that align with your values.

Discussing your plans with your loved ones can be difficult, but it is necessary to ensure that your wishes are understood and respected. Approach the topic with sensitivity and allow for an open dialogue. Your family members may have questions or emotions they need to express, and a face-to-face discussion can provide the clarity and comfort they need.

In addition to verbal communication, consider appointing a trusted executor for your death cleaning plan. This person should be organized, reliable, and willing to take on the responsibility of ensuring your wishes are fulfilled. Provide them with all the necessary documentation and information they will need to fulfill their role effectively.

Remember that the goal of Swedish death cleaning is not only to ease your burden but also to simplify the lives of those you leave behind. By communicating your plans clearly, you create a path for a smoother transition and a loving legacy that reflects your thoughtfulness and consideration.

Chapter Summary

- An essential aspect of Swedish death cleaning involves organizing legal documents and financial affairs for ease of loved ones.
- Gather and update critical legal documents like wills and trusts, informing executors and trusted individuals of their location.
- Compile a list of financial accounts, investments, insurance policies, and debts, including contact information and account details.
- Write a letter of instruction to accompany the will, providing personal guidance and sentiments.
- Document and communicate about safe deposit boxes, storage units, and valuable items.
- Consult a legal professional to ensure documents are legally sound and wishes are clear.
- Address digital assets and passwords by creating an inventory and providing access instructions.
- Estate planning and wills are essential for everyone, not just older people or the wealthy, to distribute assets and care for dependents according to one's wishes.

8

THE ART OF GIVING

In Swedish death cleaning, gift-giving becomes a thoughtful process of transferring memories and affection. As we sort through our possessions, we often come across items that may hold significant value for our loved ones while no longer serving us. This is where gift-giving intertwines with the systematic approach of death cleaning.

Ultimately, the gifts we choose to give as part of our death cleaning should be extensions of our affection and reflect our understanding of the recipient. They are tokens of our legacy, small pieces of ourselves that we entrust to others, hoping to add to their lives the richness of shared moments and lasting memories.

Choosing Meaningful Gifts for Loved Ones

Selecting gifts for our loved ones is both a gesture of affection and an expression of our legacy. To choose these gifts with intention, reflect on the relationships that have shaped our lives. Consider the individual you are gifting to: their interests, memories with you, and the message you wish to convey through this item. It is not the monetary value that defines the worth of a gift in this context but the emotional significance and the shared connection it represents. A well-chosen gift can evoke shared experiences and express understanding and appreciation.

When selecting an item, ask yourself whether it will bring joy, utility, or a sense of connection to the recipient. An heirloom, for instance, may carry the weight of family history and serve as a cherished keepsake. A book that sparked a lifelong passion, a piece of jewelry worn on a memorable occasion, or even a tool that has served you well can be a vessel for stories and sentiments you wish to pass on.

Consider also the story the item carries. A piece of jewelry may be beautiful, but it becomes truly precious when accompanied by the tale of its origin or the memories that accompanied it. Similarly, a book may hold more than the wisdom within its pages; it might also represent a shared interest or a conversation long past.

Consider the practicality of the item in the context of the recipient's life. An heirloom that requires extensive care or a large piece of furniture may not fit comfortably into their space or lifestyle. Finding a different home for these items to be fully appreciated and utilized may be more considerate. Aim for gifts that integrate seamlessly into the lives of your loved ones rather than becoming a burden. In this way, the essence of Swedish death cleaning is honored, as it seeks to lighten the load of both the giver and the receiver.

It is also important to respect the recipient's space and preferences. Open a dialogue with them to ensure your gift is welcomed and not become a burden. This conversation can be a beautiful opportunity to reminisce and reinforce bonds, making the act of giving itself a cherished memory.

The presentation of the gift can be a meaningful ritual. A handwritten note explaining the item's history and meaning in your life can significantly enhance the value of the gift. It transforms the object from a mere material possession into a narrative, a shared chapter in the story of your life and theirs.

Giving these carefully chosen items celebrates life and relationships. It is an opportunity to reflect on the bonds that have sustained us and to offer a piece of ourselves to those who will continue the story long after we are gone. Through these meaningful gifts, we can not only declutter our physical space but also enrich our emotional connection with loved ones.

Donations: Finding the Right Homes for Your Items

Donation is a meaningful and satisfying part of the death cleaning process. Donating our possessions is a way to extend their life beyond our own, to pass on the utility of the items, and to experience the spirit of generosity that comes with giving. It is essential, however, to approach this task with the same level of thoughtfulness we have applied to the rest of our cleaning.

To begin, take stock of the items you wish to donate. These could range from clothing and books to furniture and household goods. Consider the condition of each item. Donations should be in good repair, clean, and presentable. Remember, the goal is to provide something of value, not to offload the responsibility of disposal onto others.

Once you have a clear idea of what you wish to give away, the next step is to find suitable homes for your items. Research local charities and non-profit organizations that accept donations. Many organizations have specific needs or guidelines for what they can accept, so it is important to respect these requirements to ensure your items will be suitable.

Consider the potential impact of your donations. For example, donating professional attire to organizations that help individuals prepare for job interviews can significantly impact someone's life. Books can find new readers through libraries or schools, and furniture can furnish the homes of those in need.

Sometimes, you may wish to donate to specialized programs or causes close to your heart. You may have tools that could benefit a local community workshop or musical instruments that could support a school's arts program. By matching your items with the right recipients, you ensure they are appreciated and support the causes you believe in.

It's also worth considering donating to thrift stores run by charitable organizations. The proceeds from the sale of your items can support various programs and services, multiplying your contribution's impact.

When you have identified where to donate your items, organize them accordingly. Some organizations offer pick-up services; others require you to drop off your donations. Make sure to follow their processes, as this helps maintain the efficiency and effectiveness of their operations.

The act of donating should not be rushed. Take the time to reflect on the potential joy and assistance your items can bring to others. This reflection honors the spirit of döstädning and reinforces the cycle of giving and receiving that enriches our communities.

Finding the right homes for your items transforms your act of decluttering into a gesture of kindness and compassion. Through this process, we can leave a positive imprint on the world, one that resonates with the values we hold dear and the legacy we wish to leave behind.

The Impact of Your Generosity

When you choose to part with your possessions, you are both emptying space in your home and filling spaces in the lives of others. This transition of belongings from one life to another is both a physical handover and a transfer of care, respect, and generosity. Your generosity has a ripple effect that extends far beyond the initial act of giving. It touches lives in ways that are often unseen and unmeasured but deeply felt.

Consider the books that once lined your shelves, offering knowledge, escape, and comfort. In a new reader's hands, they become a source of inspiration, a catalyst for education, or a companion in solitude. The clothes you once wore, each thread woven with memories, now provide warmth and dignity to someone who may have stood vulnerable against the elements. The toys that echoed with the laughter of your children can now bring joy to another child's heart, enabling them to create their own cherished memories.

Your act of giving does not end with the physical transfer of items. It plants seeds of kindness that may bloom in unexpected ways. The recipients of your belongings may be moved to continue the cycle of generosity, passing on the items they received from you and the spirit in which they were given. In this way, your influence extends into the community, fostering a culture of giving and sharing.

The process of letting go is also a gift to yourself. It is an opportunity to reflect on what truly matters in life and to cherish the memories associated with your possessions without being anchored by them. It allows you to make peace with the impermanence of material things and to focus on the enduring nature of relationships and experiences.

The impact of your generosity is both intimate and expansive. It demonstrates the interconnectedness of our lives and the shared humanity that binds us. Through giving, you contribute to a legacy of kindness that will outlive the physical presence of the items you have parted with.

Gratitude and Reciprocity

The act of giving is a two-way street. It is a path paved with gratitude and reciprocity that enriches the experience for both the giver and the receiver. As we bestow our belongings to others, it helps to understand the raw exchange of emotions and values that occurs in this process.

Gratitude, in its purest form, is the recognition of the kindness that others have shown us. When we give away our possessions, particularly those with sentimental value, we share a piece of our life's narrative. The recipients of these items often feel a deep appreciation for the physical gift and the trust and affection it symbolizes. This gratitude is a powerful force, capable of deepening bonds and creating lasting memories.

Reciprocity, on the other hand, is the response to the gratitude felt. It is an innate human instinct to want to return kindness when it is received. Reciprocity may not always manifest in the form of physical items. Sometimes, it is the emotional support offered during the cleaning process, the shared stories about the items being passed on, or the simple act of acknowledging the effort to sort through a lifetime of belongings.

The beauty of this exchange is that it creates a cycle of goodwill that extends beyond the material. As we select items to give away, we invite others to partake in our history, and, in doing so, we also give them the opportunity to contribute to the narrative. They may reciprocate by sharing their own stories, providing companionship, or offering assistance in the practical aspects of the cleaning.

Approach this exchange without expectation, understanding that its value lies in the act itself rather than any potential return. The essence of Swedish death cleaning is to lighten the load of our existence, simplify our spaces and lives, and make our departure less burdensome for others. When we engage in this practice with a heart full of gratitude and an openness to reciprocity, we not only enrich our own lives but also bring warmth and connection to the lives of others.

As we continue to navigate the layers of belongings and memories, do so with the knowledge that each item we part with carries the potential for a meaningful exchange. The gratitude and reciprocity that flow from these acts of giving are the threads that weave the fabric of human connection, making the process of Swedish death cleaning a truly transformative experience.

Chapter Summary

- Gift-giving is a thoughtful way to pass on memories and affection to others.
- Gifts should be chosen for their emotional resonance and connection to the recipient, not monetary value.
- Respect the recipient's space and preferences, ensuring the gift is welcomed. Practicality should be considered; items requiring extensive care or space may not be suitable.
- Donating items as part of death cleaning extends their usefulness and embodies generosity. Donations should be in good condition and given to organizations where they will be valued.

- Giving has a ripple effect, fostering a culture of generosity and community support.
- Swedish death cleaning is a reciprocal process, fostering gratitude and deepening human connections.

9

OVERCOMING CHALLENGES

During your journey, you may find yourself face to face with two formidable adversaries: procrastination and overwhelm. These challenges are inherent in sorting through a lifetime's accumulation of possessions, and can be as much a part of the journey as the items themselves.

Procrastination often appears when we are confronted with tasks that seem monumental in scope. The thought of sorting through decades of belongings can be daunting, leading to a paralysis of action. It is a natural response to an overwhelming task that can be overcome with small steps and a shift in perspective.

Break the task into manageable segments to combat procrastination. Start with a single drawer, a particular category of items, or a defined space within your home. Compartmentalizing the process makes the task less intimidating, and each small victory can propel you forward. Setting aside regular, scheduled times for death cleaning can also create a routine that helps overcome the inertia that procrastination breeds.

Overwhelm, on the other hand, can engulf us when the emotional weight of our possessions comes to bear. Each object may hold a memory, sentiment, or piece of our past. The key to navigating this emotional landscape is acknowledging and permitting yourself to experience all the feelings that arise. Reflect on the significance of each item and the freedom and peace that will come from letting go.

It is also helpful to remember why you chose to do this in the first place. Was it to ease the burden on loved ones, curate a collection of items that reflect your life, or to declutter your living space and mind? Focusing on the benefits the process will bring makes it easier to push through the emotional and physical work involved.

Overwhelm can also stem from the sheer volume of items to sort through. In such cases, enlisting help from friends, family, or professionals can provide practical and emotional assistance. Sharing stories and memories as you sort through items can transform the process from a solitary chore into a shared experience, enriching the process and dispersing the weight of decision-making.

Ultimately, the journey through procrastination and feeling overwhelmed is part of the journey and requires patience and self-compassion. It is a process of revisiting the past, confronting the present, and preparing for the future. By approaching it with a reflective mindset and a systematic plan, the path becomes clearer, and the task is more approachable. With each item released, space is created—not just in the home, but in the heart and mind—for new experiences and a sense of tranquility that comes with knowing your legacy will be a blessing, not a burden.

Dealing with Resistance from Others

As you declutter your belongings, you may find that the challenge is not solely within yourself but also resistance from those around you—family, friends, and loved ones who may not immediately understand or support this process.

Resistance from others can manifest in various ways. It may come as a surprise when a family member expresses a strong emotional attachment to an item you are ready to part with, or when a friend questions the necessity of this practice, labeling it as morbid or unnecessary. These reactions are rooted in personal connections to the objects in question or from a discomfort with the concept of mortality that Swedish death cleaning inherently acknowledges.

To navigate this resistance, approach these conversations with empathy and patience. Begin by explaining the purpose and benefits of Swedish death cleaning—for yourself and those around you. Emphasize that this process is not about erasing memories but curating them, ensuring that the most significant and meaningful items are preserved without clutter.

When facing emotional attachments from others, listen and acknowledge their feelings. Engage in dialogue about the memories associated with the items and consider if there are alternative ways to honor them, such as through photographs or shared stories, rather than the physical possession itself.

In instances where resistance stems from a discomfort with the concept of death, it may be helpful to reframe the conversation around simplification and mindfulness in your current life. Swedish death cleaning is as much about living a more organized and intentional life now as it is about preparing for the future.

Setting boundaries and asserting your autonomy in the process is also beneficial. While it is important to consider the feelings of others, ultimately, the decision of what to keep and what to let go of is personal. You should gently remind others that while their input is valued, the final choices are yours.

Involving family and friends in the process can sometimes turn resistance into support. Invite them to participate in sorting through items, sharing stories, and making decisions about family heirlooms. This inclusive approach can transform the process into a collective journey, fostering understanding and inspiring others to consider their relationship with possessions.

Lastly, remember to maintain perspective. Resistance from others is often a reflection of their internal struggles and not a rejection of your efforts. You may gradually influence their perceptions and alleviate their concerns by demonstrating the positive changes and the sense of peace from Swedish death cleaning.

In the following section, we will explore how to address the physical limitations that may arise during Swedish death cleaning and the importance of seeking and accepting help when needed.

Physical Limitations and Asking for Help

Choosing to embark on the journey of Swedish death cleaning is a testament to your courage and commitment to mindful living. However, physical limitations can sometimes present significant hurdles in this process. Sorting, lifting, and organizing one's possessions can be demanding. For some, these tasks might be challenging or unfeasible due to age, health, or disability.

It is at this point that asking for help becomes necessary. The ethos of Swedish death cleaning is not to burden others with one's belongings after you pass on. Similarly, it should not burden the individual undertaking it in the present. Seeking assistance is a practical step that aligns with the spirit of the process.

When physical constraints impede your ability to carry out specific tasks, consider contacting family, friends, or professional services. This support network can provide the physical strength and endurance the task demands.

Communicate your needs and intentions clearly when asking for help. Be specific about the assistance you require, whether sorting through heavy boxes, rearranging furniture, or deciding about particular items. Those who care for you will likely appreciate the opportunity to contribute to your well-being, and the peace of mind of knowing your affairs are in order.

Respecting the boundaries and limitations of those you ask for help is equally important. Be mindful of their time and physical capabilities, and express gratitude for their assistance. If necessary, consider hiring professional help, such as a home organizer or a moving service, which can provide expertise and efficiency.

In instances where help is not readily available, it may be wise to approach the task incrementally. Break down the process into smaller, manageable tasks that align with your physical capacity. This approach not only respects your limitations but also ensures steady progress.

Swedish death cleaning is not a race against time but a thoughtful progression towards simplicity and order. It is about making the process as gentle and kind to oneself as it is to others. By acknowledging the need for help and embracing it, you honor the essence of this practice—reducing the burden on oneself and others and paving the way for a legacy of care and consideration.

Staying Motivated and Keeping Momentum

Döstädning is a process of reflection and a journey towards a tidier, more intentional living space. However, as with any journey, maintaining the drive to continue is crucial. This section will explore strategies to stay motivated and keep momentum during the decluttering process.

Firstly, set clear, achievable goals. Sorting through your possessions can be daunting, so breaking it down into smaller, more manageable tasks can make the process feel less overwhelming. Consider setting aside specific times for cleaning, perhaps an hour each day or a few hours on the weekend, and focus on one area at a time. Completing these mini-goals can provide a sense of accomplishment and encourage you to continue.

Another way to maintain motivation is to keep in mind the reasons why you started this process. Reflect on the benefits that Swedish death cleaning can bring, not only to you but also to your loved ones. The peace of mind that comes from knowing you are not leaving a burden for others can be a powerful motivator. Additionally, the act of decluttering can be liberating and can lead to a more serene living environment.

Visual progress is another motivator. Before you start, take photographs of the areas you plan to declutter. As you make progress, take new photos to document the transformation. Seeing the physical change in your space can be incredibly satisfying and spur you to continue.

Reward yourself for milestones reached. After completing a particularly challenging area, treat yourself to something enjoyable: a nice meal, a relaxing bath, or an evening with a good book. These rewards can serve as incentives to push through the more challenging parts of the cleaning process.

Finally, be patient with yourself. There will be days when

progress is slow, which is perfectly acceptable. The key is to keep moving forward, even one small step at a time.

By implementing these strategies, you can maintain motivation and momentum throughout your Swedish death cleaning journey. Each can help transform what may seem impossible into a fulfilling and life-affirming process.

Adapting the Process to Fit Your Needs

Now, let us turn our attention to the personalization of döstädning to meet your own personal needs. This process is not a one-size-fits-all endeavor; it is an intricate and individualized journey that requires adaptation to circumstances and needs.

Your life is unique, and so is your home. Your memories, possessions, and emotional attachments are yours alone. Therefore, the sorting and decluttering process should be tailored to reflect your individuality. You should craft a method that resonates with your lifestyle, values, and goals.

Begin by assessing your living space and belongings with a discerning eye. Consider the size of your home, the number of items you possess, and your physical ability to manage the task at hand. If you live in a large house with decades' worth of belongings, your approach will differ from someone in a smaller apartment. Similarly, you may need to pace yourself differently or seek assistance if you have physical limitations.

Consider your emotional readiness. Swedish death cleaning is also about confronting the emotional weight of your possessions. Some items may be easy to part with, while others may require more reflection and time. Allow yourself the flexibility to handle these items at your own pace, perhaps revisiting them after you've gained momentum with less sentimental objects.

Furthermore, your method of disposal should align with your

values. If environmental concerns are important to you, seek ways to recycle or donate items rather than discard them. If you wish to leave a legacy, consider which items might be meaningful to pass on to family members or friends and have conversations with them about these pieces.

Incorporate elements of Swedish death cleaning into your routine in a manageable way—whether that means dedicating a set amount of time each day or week to the task or integrating it into your regular cleaning schedule.

Be kind to yourself during this process. There will be moments of doubt and hesitation, but also times of clarity and liberation. By adapting the principles and strategies we've explored to fit your needs and circumstances, you create a more manageable and meaningful path for you.

Chapter Summary

- Swedish death cleaning is a decluttering process that involves emotional release and can be hindered by procrastination and overwhelm.
- Break the task into smaller segments to combat procrastination and schedule regular cleaning times.
- Overwhelm can be managed by acknowledging emotions tied to possessions and focusing on the benefits of decluttering for oneself and loved ones.
- Enlisting help from friends, family, or professionals can provide practical and emotional support during the process.
- Resistance from others may occur; approach these situations with empathy, patience, and clear communication about the purpose of death cleaning.

- Physical limitations may require asking for help from others or hiring professional services to assist with the cleaning process.
- Staying motivated involves setting clear goals, involving others, documenting progress, rewarding oneself, and being patient.
- The cleaning process should be personalized to fit your needs, considering your living space, physical ability, emotional readiness, and values.

10

LIFE AFTER DEATH CLEANING

We have traversed through the philosophical underpinnings and the practical steps of decluttering your life in preparation to create a simpler, clutter-free future. It is now time to reflect on the transformative impact this process can have on our day-to-day existence. Reducing our possessions involves a conscious choice to embrace a minimalist lifestyle.

At its core, minimalism is about paring down life to its essentials. It is a deliberate decision to eschew the material in favor of what truly adds value to our lives. In Swedish death cleaning, minimalism takes on a poignant significance. It is about creating a serene environment that reflects our most cherished values, making room for the activities and relationships that enrich our existence.

The freedom that comes with living with less is multifaceted. Fewer possessions mean less time and energy spent on cleaning, maintenance, and organization. This newfound time can be redirected towards hobbies, passions, or simply the joy of leisure. It is a liberation from the relentless pursuit of material acquisitions that often defines modern life.

Physically, the spaces we inhabit become more open and tranquil. There is a tangible peace that comes with the absence of excess. Rooms are easier to navigate, clean, and maintain, saving time and reducing the stress associated with household chores. This simplicity in our surroundings can lead to a more serene lifestyle, where the emphasis is on living, not maintaining possessions.

Psychologically, the benefits are equally far-reaching. A minimalist lifestyle can lead to a clearer mind, reduced anxiety, and a greater sense of control. In the absence of clutter, there is space for clarity and focus. The mind, no longer preoccupied with the chaos of clutter, can focus more readily on the present moment, fostering a state of mindfulness often elusive in a world of material distractions. The things we keep around us gain greater significance, and we become more mindful of what we allow into our personal space.

Emotionally, the freedom of living with less can be liberating. The ties to the past, often embodied in the form of material goods, can be gently severed, allowing for a forward-looking perspective. This is not to say that all memories or sentimental items are discarded, but rather that a selective process helps to prioritize what truly matters. The emotional weight of objects is acknowledged, but it no longer anchors us to a bygone era.

Embracing minimalism can also have a positive impact on our relationships. We can foster deeper connections with our loved ones with fewer distractions and less emphasis on material wealth. It encourages us to value experiences over objects, creating memories that outlast any physical item.

Financially, the minimalist approach Swedish death cleaning advocates can lead to a more sustainable way of living. Buying less and choosing quality over quantity can reduce our ecological footprint and contribute to a more ethical consumer culture. The savings accrued from this lifestyle can be allocated to more meaningful pursuits or set aside for future security.

Swedish death cleaning is not a singular event, but a continuous practice that encourages us to evaluate our belongings and our attachment to them regularly. This ongoing process helps to cultivate a sense of detachment from material goods, reinforcing the idea that our worth is not measured by what we own but by the richness of our experiences and relationships.

The benefits of living with less extend beyond the individual to the communal and environmental levels. By consuming and hoarding less, we contribute to a culture of sustainability that values resources and reduces the ecological footprint left behind for future generations. It is a conscious choice to partake in a lifestyle that respects the finite nature of our planet's resources.

The minimalist lifestyle that emerges from Swedish death cleaning is about making intentional choices. It is a commitment to live with purpose and to recognize that our possessions do not define us. As we continue to explore the implications of this transformative cleaning process, it becomes clear that letting go involves more than just preparing for our departure from this world. It is also about enhancing the quality of our lives while we are here, creating a legacy of simplicity and intentionality.

In embracing the freedom of living with less, we find that our lives are not diminished but enhanced. The space we create by letting go of the unnecessary allows for new experiences, relationships, and opportunities to enter. It is a space that breathes, grows, and adapts with us as we continue our journey through life, ever mindful of the legacy we wish to leave behind.

Continuing the Practices of Döstädning

Embracing the principles of döstädning is a transformative lifestyle choice that extends beyond the initial clutter purge. This philosophy, rooted in practicality and mindfulness, encourages a continuous cycle of evaluating the necessity and emotional value of our possessions. By integrating the practices of döstädning into our daily lives, we not only prepare for the eventual ease of our passing but also cultivate an environment that reflects a life of intention and clarity.

To continue the practices of döstädning, one must adopt a reflective approach to consumption and possession. This means regularly assessing items for their current utility and emotional significance. The question, "Will anyone I know be happier if I save this?" becomes a guiding mantra, prompting thoughtful decision-making. It's about recognizing that our belongings have a lifecycle, much like ourselves, and being at peace with letting go when the time is right.

An organized system is also key to maintaining the principles of döstädning. This involves setting aside time, perhaps seasonally or annually, to revisit each space in your home. During these times, you can re-evaluate items that may have slipped back into obscurity, ensuring that everything you own remains purposeful or cherished. It's not about creating a stark or sterile environment but about maintaining a harmonious space filled only with items that serve a positive function in your life.

Keeping your personal documents, accounts, and legal matters in order is an ongoing process that requires regular attention. This ensures that, in the event of one's passing, the practical aspects of dealing with their estate are as straightforward and unburdened by complication as possible.

In this way, the practices of döstädning offer a form of self-care that extends to caring for those we will one day leave behind. It is a thoughtful and continuous process of considering our material legacy and the impact it will have on our loved ones. By choosing to live with less and being intentional about what we keep in our lives, we free ourselves from the physical weight of unnecessary possessions and the mental and emotional burdens they can represent.

As we journey through life, embracing the simplicity and foresight that döstädning provides, we find that the benefits of this practice are not confined to the end of life. The peace of mind and freedom that come from a decluttered and well-ordered environment enhance our daily existence, allowing us to live more fully in the present while thoughtfully preparing for the future.

Sharing Your Experience and Inspiring Others

As you continue on the transformative journey of Swedish death cleaning, you may find that the impact of this practice extends far beyond the confines of your own home and personal space. The process of mindfully decluttering and organizing your possessions in anticipation of life's final chapter is not only a gift to yourself but also to those who will carry on after you. It is a profound act of love and consideration that can inspire and guide others in their journeys toward simplicity and intentionality.

Sharing your experience of death cleaning with friends, family, and even broader communities can be a powerful way to extend the benefits of this practice. It is not uncommon for individuals who have undergone döstädning to feel a sense of liberation and peace, which can be contagious. When you talk about the emotional relief and clarity that comes from letting go of unnecessary belongings, you may notice a spark of interest or recognition in your listeners' eyes.

Consider how you can communicate your story. You may start with casual conversations, where you can discuss the positive changes you've noticed in your daily life. You could share anecdotes about items that held special memories and how you chose to honor those memories, whether by keeping, gifting, or thoughtfully disposing of those items.

For those more inclined to engage with larger audiences, writing a blog post, hosting a workshop, or even starting a support group could be effective ways to spread the philosophy and practical steps of Swedish death cleaning. In these settings, you can delve deeper into the emotional aspects of the process, the challenges you faced, and the strategies you employed to overcome them.

It's important to approach these discussions with sensitivity and understanding, as death cleaning can evoke many emotions, from apprehension to curiosity. By sharing your own vulnerabilities and learning experiences, you create a safe space for others to explore their feelings and questions about the practice.

Being open about your difficulties and how you addressed them provides a realistic perspective to help others set reasonable expectations for their death cleaning journey. Your unique approach to sorting through belongings, deciding what to keep, and finding new homes for items you no longer need can serve as a blueprint for others.

Remember that your story has the power to motivate change. As people in your circle begin to see the tangible results of your efforts—perhaps a more organized living space, a lighter emotional load, or a renewed sense of purpose—they may be encouraged to embark on their own paths of mindful decluttering.

In sharing your experience, you are not only recounting a personal tale of decluttering and preparation but also imparting a philosophy of living with intention. Swedish death cleaning is as much about examining one's life and values as it is about physical possessions. Inspiring others to consider what is important contributes to a broader cultural shift toward mindfulness and sustainability.

Sharing your experience with Swedish death cleaning is an extension of the practice itself. It is an opportunity to reflect on the journey, to consolidate the lessons learned, and to offer guidance to those who may one day walk a similar path. Your story, woven from practicality, reflection, and systematic planning, will inspire others as they navigate the complexities of their own lives, possessions, and the legacy they wish to leave behind.

The Ongoing Journey of Self-Discovery

Swedish death cleaning is a transformative journey into the heart of who we are, what we value, and how we wish to be remembered. As we declutter the layers of our material possessions, we are often confronted with the layers of our identity, peeling back the years and the memories that have defined us.

Organizing and letting go of our physical belongings can be a very introspective experience. Each object, whether a treasured photograph, a well-worn book, or a seemingly insignificant trinket, holds a mirror up to our lives, reflecting the moments we've lived and the emotions we've felt. In this way, Swedish death cleaning transcends its practical purposes and catalyzes self-discovery.

As we continue on this path, our relationship with our possessions shifts. What once seemed indispensable may now appear redundant. We learn to distinguish between what genuinely enriches our lives and what merely occupies space. This understanding extends beyond the physical realm; it influences our choices, relationships, and sense of purpose. We start to prioritize experiences over objects, quality over quantity, and meaningful connections over fleeting interactions.

This process often prompts us to consider our legacy. What are the stories we want to tell? What wisdom do we hope to impart? And what would we like to leave behind, not just in terms of physical items, but in the memories and impacts we've had on others? It is in this way that Swedish death cleaning also becomes about refining the quality of our living.

In embracing the principles of Swedish death cleaning, we embark on a continuous journey of self-discovery. It is a process that does not end with the last discarded item but evolves with us. With each object we release, we reaffirm our values and vision for the life we desire. In this ongoing practice, we find a sense of preparedness for our eventual departure and a deeper appreciation for the present moment and the transient beauty of life itself.

Chapter Summary

- Swedish death cleaning is a decluttering philosophy that prepares for death and embraces minimalism. Minimalism involves focusing on essentials, valuing experiences over possessions, and creating a serene environment.
- Living with fewer possessions can lead to less time spent on maintenance and more on hobbies and relationships.

- A minimalist lifestyle can reduce anxiety, increase focus, and improve financial sustainability.
- Regularly practicing Swedish death cleaning can help maintain a decluttered space and keep personal affairs in order.
- Sharing experiences of death cleaning can inspire others to adopt a minimalist lifestyle and focus on what's important.
- The process is about physical decluttering, self-discovery, and considering one's legacy.
- Swedish death cleaning is an ongoing journey that enhances the present and prepares for the future.

THE LASTING IMPACT OF SWEDISH DEATH CLEANING

As we approach the conclusion of our exploration into the practice of Swedish death cleaning, let us pause and reflect upon the personal transformation that accompanies this journey. The process, which began as a practical endeavor to declutter and organize one's possessions in preparation for the inevitable, often evolves into a profound exercise in self-discovery and personal growth.

Throughout the chapters of this book, we have discovered the various aspects of Swedish death cleaning, from its pragmatic steps to its emotional nuances. Now, as we stand at the final chapter, it is time to turn our gaze inward and contemplate the internal changes that have taken place.

For many, sorting through a lifetime's worth of belongings extends beyond physical tidiness; it becomes about reconciling one's history. Each object, whether kept, discarded, or passed on, carries a narrative, a fragment of one's identity. Through death cleaning, individuals often encounter forgotten memories, confront unresolved emotions, and reconnect with their past selves. This confrontation with one's life story can lead to a sense of closure and peace as if by organizing our external world, we inadvertently arrange the scattered pieces of our inner world.

Swedish death cleaning prompts us to reevaluate what truly holds value in our lives. As we sift through the material possessions surrounding us, we are compelled to ask ourselves which items serve a purpose and which merely occupy space. This understanding extends beyond the physical realm; it encourages a broader contemplation of our priorities, relationships, and the legacy we wish to leave behind. It is common for many to emerge from this process with a renewed focus on the quality of their connections and experiences rather than the quantity of their possessions.

The introspective nature of death cleaning also fosters a heightened awareness of mortality. While this may initially seem unsettling, it often leads to a more intentional approach to living. Recognizing the impermanence of life can inspire us to make the most of our time, cherish the present, and act with purpose and kindness. The clarity gained from contemplating our finitude can be a powerful catalyst for living a life aligned with our deepest values.

In embracing the principles of Swedish death cleaning, we inadvertently embark on a journey of self-improvement. The lessons learned extend far beyond the confines of our homes and into the essence of our being. As we declutter our physical spaces, we simultaneously clear the way for personal growth, allowing for new experiences, insights, and a deeper understanding of ourselves.

Consider how this personal transformation can ripple outward, influencing not only our own lives but also the lives of those around us. The impact of Swedish death cleaning, as we will explore in the following pages, can reach far beyond the individual, touching the lives of family, friends, and the broader community.

The Ripple Effect on Family and Community

Swedish death cleaning is not merely a solitary act of decluttering or organizing one's possessions in anticipation of life's final chapter. It is a process that extends beyond the individual, touching the lives of everyone around them in lasting ways.

When someone begins the journey of Swedish death cleaning, they are often motivated by the desire to ease the burden on their loved ones after their passing. This thoughtful gesture, however, has a ripple effect that goes beyond the practicalities of minimizing possessions. It can transform relationships as family members engage in conversations about the significance of various items, sharing stories and memories that might otherwise have remained unspoken. These dialogues often lead to a deeper understanding and appreciation of one's heritage and family history, strengthening bonds and fostering a sense of continuity.

Swedish death cleaning can inspire others to reflect on their consumption habits and the accumulation of material goods. As family members witness the benefits of living with less and the peace of mind that comes with a decluttered space, they may be encouraged to embark on their journeys of simplification. This can lead to a collective shift towards more mindful living, focusing on the quality of experiences rather than the quantity of possessions.

The community at large can also benefit from Swedish death cleaning. Items that someone no longer needs or wants can find new life with others who may need them. Donations to local charities, second-hand stores, and community centers extend the usefulness of these items and support the welfare of others within the community. Giving can foster a spirit of generosity and interconnectedness, reminding us that our actions can contribute to the well-being of those around us.

Furthermore, the environmental impact of Swedish death cleaning should not be overlooked. Individuals contribute to a more sustainable way of living by consciously choosing to downsize and recycle. This can lead to a greater awareness of environmental issues within the community and encourage collective efforts to reduce waste and promote responsible consumption.

Swedish death cleaning is more than a method for organizing one's physical belongings; it catalyzes positive change that resonates through families and communities. It prompts us to consider the material legacy we leave behind and the emotional and social imprint we make on the world. It reminds us that the choices we make today can shape the lives of others and the communities we are a part of long after we are gone.

Envisioning Your Legacy

Swedish death cleaning encourages us to envision the mark we want to leave on the world and how we want to be remembered by those who survive us.

Legacy is a tapestry woven from the threads of our actions, choices, and the material echoes we leave behind. Döstädning is a deliberate and thoughtful approach to shaping the narrative of our lives as perceived by future generations. It is about creating a curated collection of our existence that highlights the values and relationships we hold dear.

In paring down our belongings, we can reassess our life's narrative. What are the items that truly matter? Which objects tell the story of who we are and the life we've lived? By keeping what is meaningful, we allow our legacy to shine through the clutter of everyday existence. This is not about erasing our presence but distilling it to its essence, ensuring that what remains reflects our self.

This process is an act of kindness and consideration. It is a way to ease the burden on our loved ones, sparing them the daunting task of sifting through our possessions in a time of grief. It is a final act of care, a way to gently guide them through the remnants of our lives, making mourning and remembrance a little less overwhelming.

Swedish death cleaning is a ritual that helps us confront our mortality with grace and intention, allowing us to leave behind a meaningful and considerate legacy. It is a final gift to those we love, a way to say, "I cared enough to make this easier for you."

As you move forward, carry with you the understanding that the clarity and simplicity you create through this process can serve as a guiding light for your loved ones. It is a way to say farewell with mindfulness and respect, ensuring that our departure is as clean and ordered as the life we strove to lead.

Closing Thoughts and Gratitude

As we conclude our exploration into the thoughtful practice of Swedish death cleaning, it is fitting to pause and reflect on the everlasting effects this tradition can have on our lives and those we leave behind. Decluttering and organizing our possessions with the end in mind is both a practical endeavor and a deeply emotional and spiritual journey that touches the core of our human experience.

Döstädning transcends the simple act of tidying up. It is a deliberate and purposeful way of reviewing one's life, acknowledging the impermanence of our existence, and expressing gratitude for the objects and memories that have accompanied us along the way. Through this lens, each item we choose to pass on or let go of becomes a testament to our lives and our connections.

In practicing Swedish death cleaning, we offer a final gift to our loved ones: the gift of simplicity. By curating our belongings, we alleviate the burden that might otherwise fall on family and friends during a time of grief. This act of service is imbued with love and consideration, ensuring that our departure is not overshadowed by the daunting task of sorting through all of our accumulated belongings.

This process can be a catalyst for expressing gratitude for the myriad experiences that have shaped us. As we sift through our belongings, we can recount our stories, share our history, and impart the wisdom we have gained. This can be an incredibly meaningful exchange between generations, as cherished heirlooms and personal anecdotes are passed down, keeping our legacy alive.

Swedish death cleaning prompts us to live more intentionally in the present. By regularly assessing what we own and why we own it, we become more mindful of our consumption and the footprint we leave behind. This heightened awareness can lead to a more sustainable and purposeful lifestyle that values quality over quantity and experiences over possessions.

In gratitude, we must acknowledge that Swedish death cleaning is not just about preparing for the end. It is about enhancing the quality of our current existence by creating a harmonious and clutter-free environment that allows us to focus on what truly matters. It is about living with intention and leaving with grace.

As we close this chapter, let us embody the lessons of Swedish death cleaning with a sense of peace and preparedness. May we approach the future and the end of our days with the same care and dignity with which we have lived our lives thus far, and may the legacy we leave be as orderly and serene as the spaces we have curated.

THE ESSENTIAL GUIDE TO AGING WITH GRACE

HOW TO LIVE A MORE MEANINGFUL LIFE BY EMBRACING LIFE'S TRANSITIONS AND AGING GRACEFULLY

EMBRACING THE GOLDEN YEARS

As the sun traces its arc from dawn to dusk, so too does the human life cycle extend from the energetic morning of youth through the fullness of midday maturity and gently into the twilight of the golden years. This aging journey is as natural as the changing seasons, an inevitable passage that carries a wealth of experience, wisdom, and a deepened appreciation for life's fleeting beauty.

To age is to have danced with time, felt its rhythm in our bones, and seen its colors etched upon our faces. It is a process that does not ask for our permission; it simply unfolds, day by day. Yet, how we navigate this journey—how we embrace the changes and adapt to the shifting landscapes of our lives—speaks volumes about who we are and what we value.

Aging with grace is not about denying the passage of time or the transformations it brings. Instead, it is about moving through the years with dignity, self-respect, and an unwavering spirit. It is about cultivating resilience and finding joy in the present moment, even as we honor the memories that have shaped us. It is about maintaining our sense of purpose and continuing to contribute to the world around us in meaningful ways.

As we embark on this exploration of aging with grace, we acknowledge the diversity of experiences that come with growing older. Each person's path is unique, marked by individual triumphs and trials, health and vitality, or the need for care and support. But a common thread binds us—a shared humanity that seeks connection, understanding, and the gentle acceptance of ourselves and others as we are, not as we once were.

The following chapters will delve into the myriad aspects of aging with grace. We will explore the attitudes, practices, and lifestyle choices that can help us accept and celebrate our passing years. We will consider how society, culture, and our perceptions influence the way we age.

By approaching aging as a natural, dignified, and immensely valuable stage of life, we open ourselves to the profound lessons it has to offer. We learn to let go of the trivial and to embrace the essential. We discover that while our physical strength may wane, our capacity for love, empathy, and understanding can flourish. In this way, aging becomes not a decline but a culmination—a time to harvest the fruits of a well-lived life and share their sweetness with the world.

What Does Aging with Grace Mean?

To age with grace is to accept the passage of time as an ally, not an enemy. It is a conscious choice to live life with dignity, positivity, and fulfillment, regardless of the years that pass.

Aging with grace is not solely about maintaining physical health or the ability to engage in activities without impediment, although these are important aspects. It's about cultivating an inner resilience that allows us to face the changes and challenges that come with each new chapter of life. It's about the poise and confidence with which we carry our past experiences and the wisdom we have gleaned from them.

This concept transcends the superficial focus on youth and beauty that society often emphasizes and instead honors the depth of character, the strength of spirit, and the continuity of personal growth. To age with grace is to wear your years with pride, not as a burden, but as a badge of honor proclaiming, "I have lived, I have learned, and I continue to grow."

It involves a harmonious balance between accepting the inevitable physical transformations that come with aging and nurturing the mental and emotional aspects of our being. It's about staying connected with others, engaging with the world in meaningful ways, and allowing oneself to adapt elegantly to the ever-evolving dance of life.

At its core, aging with grace is about attitude. It's a mindset that embraces the present while respecting the past and looking forward to the future. It's about living authentically, expressing gratitude for the journey thus far, and maintaining a sense of curiosity and openness to the experiences yet to come.

In this light, aging becomes not a process of diminishment but enrichment. Each year adds layers to our story, offering opportunities to refine our understanding of ourselves and the world around us. It's a chance to share our legacy, impart the lessons we've learned, and touch the lives of others with the gentle hand of earned insight.

As we move forward, let us consider how we can challenge the stereotypes and misconceptions that often cloud the true beauty of aging. By doing so, we empower ourselves and reshape the cultural narrative for generations to follow.

Challenging Age-Related Stereotypes

Each experience in our lives contributes to the richness of our personal narratives. As we weave our way into the golden years, it's essential to recognize that aging is not merely a biological process but a complex interplay of culture, perception, and individual stories. To age with grace is to understand and challenge the age-related stereotypes that often color our society's views on growing older.

Stereotypes about aging are deeply ingrained in many cultures, painting the later stages of life with broad strokes of decline and diminished value. These stereotypes suggest that age brings an inevitable loss of beauty, vitality, and relevance. However, such ideas fail to acknowledge the diversity of experiences and the potential for growth, wisdom, and continued contribution that can flourish in later years.

Challenging these stereotypes begins with recognizing their presence and the subtle ways they influence our attitudes and behaviors toward aging. It's about questioning the media portrayals that often depict older individuals as out of touch or burdensome and, instead, celebrating the myriad ways they enrich our communities. It's about shifting the narrative from one of loss to one of opportunity and continued evolution.

To confront and dismantle these stereotypes, we must start with self-reflection. How do we perceive our own aging process? Are we adopting these societal views unconsciously, or are we actively defining what aging means to us on our own terms? By cultivating a personal understanding of aging rooted in respect, self-compassion, and an appreciation for the journey, we set the stage for a more inclusive and empowering dialogue about what it means to grow older.

We must also consider the language we use when discussing aging. Words have power, and the terms we choose can either perpetuate stereotypes or help to dismantle them. By using language that emphasizes the positive aspects of aging and the individuality of each person's experience, we contribute to a culture that values and respects older adults.

In our communities, challenging age-related stereotypes means creating spaces that are inclusive and accessible to people of all ages. It means providing opportunities for intergenerational connection, where the wisdom of older adults is not only recognized but sought after. It involves advocating for policies that support older individuals' health, well-being, and engagement, ensuring that they are not marginalized but celebrated as integral members of society.

As we embrace the golden years, we come to understand that aging is a privilege denied to many. By challenging the stereotypes that have long defined what it means to grow older, we open the door to a world where every stage of life is valued and where aging with grace is possible for everyone.

The Importance of Mindset in Aging

As we journey through life, our mindset is the compass that guides our experiences and interpretations of the world around us. This is especially true as we enter the golden years, a period which can be as rich and fulfilling as any other chapter of our lives. How we approach aging can profoundly influence not only our well-being but also how society perceives and values the later stages of life.

Aging with grace is not about denying the passage of time or the changes it brings. Instead, it is about embracing these years with a positive and proactive attitude. It is about recognizing that while our bodies may evolve and our pace may slow, our zest for life and capacity for doesn't need to diminish. Our mindset can be our most powerful ally in this process, transforming how we live daily.

Mindset is more important than you might imagine when it comes to aging. Those who view aging as an opportunity for continued growth and learning tend to lead more satisfying lives. They are more likely to stay active, engage with their communities, and maintain strong relationships with friends and family. This perspective fosters resilience, enabling individuals to adapt to age-related changes gracefully and with dignity.

A positive mindset can also have tangible health benefits. Research suggests that individuals with optimistic outlooks may experience better physical health, including lower rates of chronic disease and a longer lifespan. The mind-body connection is particularly evident in how stress and happiness affect our physiological state. By cultivating a mindset that emphasizes the positives of aging, we have the power to enhance our overall health and vitality.

Maintaining a positive mindset is not always easy. Life can present challenges that test our resolve and shake our confidence. However, the beauty of the human spirit lies in its resilience and capacity for hope. By learning to adapt our mindset, we can approach these challenges not as insurmountable obstacles but as enriching experiences.

In this book, we will explore the various facets of aging with grace, from the practical strategies that can help maintain physical and mental health to the deeper philosophical reflections on the meaning and purpose of this stage of life.

As we move forward, let us hold onto the understanding that our mindset is a choice that we can shape and refine over time. It is a source of empowerment, allowing us to approach the golden years not with trepidation but with anticipation for the opportunities and wisdom they bring. With each passing year, we have the chance to redefine what it means to live fully, contribute meaningfully, and age with undeniable grace.

Overview of the Book's Journey

In this book, we will embark on a deeply personal and universally relevant journey. This book is a tapestry woven with wisdom, practical advice, and heartfelt insights that will illuminate the path to aging with grace.

In the chapters that lie ahead, we will explore the multifaceted aspects of growing older. We will delve into the importance of maintaining physical health, not only as a means of prolonging life but as a way to enhance the quality of every day. We'll discover how regular exercise, a balanced diet, and preventive healthcare can become pillars of a vibrant later life.

But aging with grace is not solely a physical endeavor. Our mental and emotional well-being are equally crucial. We will explore how lifelong learning, creative pursuits, and social connections contribute to a resilient and fulfilled mind. We will address the challenges often accompanying aging, such as loss and loneliness, and offer compassionate strategies for navigating these experiences with dignity and strength.

As we progress, we will also consider the spiritual dimension of aging. Regardless of individual beliefs or religious affiliations, many find that the golden years are a time for reflection, growth, and a deepening sense of purpose. We will share insights on cultivating a sense of inner peace and finding joy in the present moment, even as we honor the past and look to the future.

This book will not shy away from the practicalities of aging. We'll provide guidance on financial planning, healthcare decisions, and the legal considerations that can help ensure your wishes are respected and your legacy is secured. We will discuss how to create a living environment that supports your changing needs, whether adapting to your current home or considering new living arrangements.

Throughout this journey, we will learn that, while each person's path is unique, there are commonalities that bind us in our shared human experience.

This book is an invitation to embrace the golden years with an open heart and a proactive spirit. It is a guide for those who aspire to age with a sense of purpose and triumph. Together, we will discover that the later chapters of life can be among the most rewarding and that aging with grace is not only possible but profoundly enriching.

Chapter Summary

- Aging is a natural and inevitable process that brings experience, wisdom, and a deeper appreciation for life.
- Embracing aging with grace involves dignity, resilience, and finding joy in the present while contributing meaningfully to society.
- Aging with grace transcends superficial societal focuses on youth and beauty, emphasizing character, spirit, and personal growth.
- Challenging age-related stereotypes involves recognizing their influence and promoting a positive, inclusive view of aging.
- A positive mindset towards aging can lead to better physical health, satisfaction, and resilience in facing life's challenges.

- This book will explore attitudes, practices, and lifestyle choices that celebrate aging and challenge societal stereotypes. We'll also cover insights relating to physical health, mental and emotional well-being, spiritual growth, and practical considerations for aging.

1

HEALTH AND WELLNESS: THE FOUNDATIONS OF VITALITY

Our bodies undergo various changes over the years. Nutrition, the fuel that sustains us, becomes increasingly significant as we age. Nutrition powers our vitality and the sustenance that can either support or undermine the grace with which we navigate our later years.

Imagine the body as a vessel on a voyage; to maintain its integrity against the tides of time, it requires a diet rich in nutrients and considerate of its evolving needs. The aging body is a refined instrument that responds best to quality over quantity. It's not just about what we eat but how we nourish the intricate biological systems that have supported us throughout our lives.

As we delve into the essence of nutrition for the aging body, we must acknowledge the importance of balance and moderation. The palette of foods we choose should paint a picture of diversity, incorporating fruits, vegetables, whole grains, lean proteins, and healthy fats. These elements help reduce inflammation, bolster immunity, and enhance cognitive function—critical components to aging with poise.

Antioxidants emerge as the guardians in this nutritional landscape, their presence in colorful fruits and vegetables helping to protect cells from the oxidative stress that can accelerate aging. Omega-3 fatty acids in fish, flaxseeds, and walnuts serve as lubricants for our cardiovascular system, keeping the heart's rhythm steady and strong.

As we age, our bodies may not absorb nutrients as efficiently as they once did, so adjustments may need to be made to our diet. Focusing on nutrient-dense foods that deliver the maximum benefit without excessive calories becomes ever more important. The role of vitamins and minerals—such as calcium and vitamin D for bone health, B vitamins for energy metabolism, and vitamin C for skin elasticity—is paramount.

Hydration holds a place of honor in the body's diet. Water is essential for maintaining cellular health, aiding digestion, and preventing kidney function decline. A simple act of drinking adequate water can have profound effects on well-being.

We must not forget the social and emotional dimensions of eating. Meals are a source of sustenance and a ritual of connection, a time to gather with loved ones to share stories and laughter. The joy derived from these moments can nourish the soul as much as food nourishes the body.

Ultimately, fueling the aging body is about extending and enriching our years and crafting a diet that supports a life of activity, engagement, and fulfillment. With each mindful choice at the table, we are not merely eating but composing the later chapters of our lives with intention and care.

Carry with you the understanding that the foods we choose are the building blocks for a resilient, vibrant body. With this foundation of health and wellness, we are better prepared to embrace the activities that keep both body and mind active, which we will explore in the following pages.

Exercise: Keeping the Body and Mind Active

Our bodies and minds will always seek the nourishment of movement, much like they crave the sustenance of a well-balanced meal. In all its different forms, exercise is an essential component of a vibrant life. It is a fountain of energy that flows within reach, offering vitality to those willing to partake in its benefits.

Staying active is vital to maintaining and improving our health as we age, helping us pursue a long life and enhance the quality of every year we live. Regular exercise bolsters our physical strength, supports cardiovascular health, and helps manage weight. But its benefits extend beyond the physical; it also nurtures the mind, offering clarity and resilience against the stresses of life.

Engaging in physical activity does not require strenuous workouts or gym memberships. It is about finding joy in the movement and integrating it into our daily lives. For some, this may mean taking brisk walks in the park, where the fresh air and the beauty of nature can also soothe the soul. For others, it might involve joining a dance class, where the rhythm of music and the camaraderie of other fellow dancers create a symphony of well-being.

Strength training can also play a vital role, particularly in combating the loss of muscle mass that naturally occurs with age. Resistance exercises, whether with weights or through body-weight movements like yoga or Pilates, can help maintain and build muscle strength. This not only helps you perform everyday tasks but also protects against injury, ensuring that your body remains robust and resilient.

Balance and flexibility exercises are equally important, as they help prevent falls—a common concern as we age. Practices such as tai chi or simple balance exercises at home can significantly improve your stability and agility, fostering confidence in movement.

Exercise also has a positive impact on cognitive health. Studies have shown that regular physical activity can improve memory, attention, and processing speed. It can even contribute to the growth of new brain cells, a process once thought impossible in older adults. By engaging in exercise, we are caring for our bodies and investing in our minds' sharpness and vitality.

As we integrate exercise into our lives, we must listen to our bodies and respect their limits. This is neither a race nor a finish line to cross. Exercise is a personal journey that should be approached with patience and self-compassion. Starting small, achievable sessions and gradually building intensity and duration can lead to a sustainable and enjoyable exercise routine.

In the end, moving our bodies is an act of honoring them. It is a celebration of what they can do, regardless of age. Exercise is a powerful ally in the art of aging with grace, a regular practice that can infuse each moment with energy and purpose. Exercise revitalizes the body and the spirit, setting the stage for a life of vitality and joy.

Mental Health: Cultivating a Resilient Mind

As we get older and accumulate more and more life experiences, we must also focus our attention on our mental health and well-being. Aging with grace is more than a physical endeavor; it is profoundly intertwined with our mental health. Cultivating a resilient mind can help us handle life's ups and downs with calmness and strength.

Resilience is the ability to bounce back from life's stress, adversity, and challenges. It enables us to face our days with composure and recover from setbacks with our spirits intact. As we age, this resilience helps us deal with life's challenges with a sense of intention and happiness.

A rich and active social life can help you build this resilience. The bonds we form with family, friends, and community provide a network of support that can offer comfort and assistance when we need it most. These relationships nourish our need for connection and belonging, which are as fundamental to our well-being as the air we breathe.

Engaging in activities challenging and stimulating the mind is another key to maintaining mental agility. Whether learning a new language, taking up an instrument, or simply indulging in puzzles and games, these pursuits help keep the mind sharp and can even reduce cognitive decline. They offer a sense of accomplishment and progress, reminding us that growth is possible at any age.

Mindfulness and meditation are also powerful tools for mental health. We learn to observe our thoughts and feelings without judgment by anchoring ourselves in the present moment. This practice can reduce stress, enhance emotional regulation, and deepen our understanding of ourselves and our place in the world.

Acknowledging and addressing the emotional challenges that may arise as we age is equally important. Grief, loss, and change are natural parts of life's cycle, and seeking support through therapy or counseling can be an act of courage and self-care. These resources provide a space to process our experiences and emotions, allowing us to move forward with grace and wisdom.

Finally, laughter and happiness are essential ingredients in the recipe of life. Finding humor in life's quirks, enjoying the company of loved ones, and embracing the simple pleasures each day offers are simple activities that can also be immensely healing. These moments of lightness contribute to a more resilient mindset, reminding us that amidst life's ebb and flow, there is always space for happiness and hope.

A resilient mind complements and enhances our overall well-being, and a harmonious balance between body and mind supports a life of vitality and grace. Mental resilience is about enduring and thriving, with every sunrise bringing new opportunities for growth and contentment.

Sleep: The Cornerstone of Recovery

Getting enough sleep is crucial because it helps us heal and stay young at heart. During the calmness of night, our bodies undertake the vital work of rejuvenation, allowing us to greet each new day with renewed energy and vitality.

When we sleep, it's not just our body that heals; our brain and cognitive function also need this time to restore itself. Sleep is intricately linked to memory consolidation, where the experiences and knowledge of the day are processed and stored. As we age, this nightly ritual becomes even more crucial, as it supports cognitive health and helps maintain clarity and quickness of mind.

Understanding the changes in sleep patterns as we age is key to embracing this natural progression with grace. It is not uncommon for older adults to experience changes in their sleep routine, such as taking longer to fall asleep, waking up more frequently during the night, and experiencing a shift toward earlier bed and wake times. These changes are all a normal part of aging and are closely linked to a good night's rest.

Consider how you use your bedroom to foster the best possible sleep environment. This space should be a tranquil haven reserved for sleep and intimacy alone. Removing electronic devices, embracing comfortable bedding, and maintaining a cool, dark, and quiet atmosphere can all contribute to a more conducive sleep setting.

Establishing a consistent sleep routine can signal to your body that it is time to wind down. Gentle rituals before bed, such as a warm bath, reading a book, or practicing relaxation techniques, can ease the transition into sleep. It is also wise to be mindful of diet and exercise; a light evening meal and regular physical activity can promote better sleep, though vigorous exercise should be avoided close to bedtime.

If you find sleeping difficult, approach this challenge patiently and seek guidance when needed. Sometimes, underlying health issues or medications can interfere with sleep, and in such cases, consulting with a healthcare professional can lead to solutions that restore the natural balance of your nocturnal rhythms.

In the symphony of our later years, sleep is the silent interlude that allows our days to be lived with passion and purpose. By honoring the importance of sleep in our daily lives, we not only enhance our physical and mental well-being but also embrace the opportunity to age with the grace and dignity that each of us deserves.

Preventative Care: Staying Ahead of Health Challenges

Another component of aging with grace lies in anticipating and navigating the health challenges you may face over time. It is in this spirit that we explore the concept of preventative care. This proactive approach helps guide us through the uncertainty of potential health concerns.

Taking care of your health early means looking ahead and caring for your body and mind before small health issues become big problems. Preventative care is like a silent guard protecting our health and keeping us strong as we age. This approach to health is not about fearing what might come but recognizing what can be done now to maintain vitality and vigor.

To avoid health challenges, embrace a lifestyle that supports your body's natural defenses. This includes a balanced diet rich in nutrients, which fuel our cells and the building blocks for repair and regeneration. Regular physical activity, tailored to your abilities and interests, keeps the muscles strong and the heart resilient while nurturing the mind with a sense of accomplishment and joy.

Preventative care involves regular health screenings and checkups, which help keep the body in check. These check-ins with healthcare professionals are invaluable because they can detect subtle changes that may signal the need for intervention. Finding health problems early contributes to aging well because it usually means more straightforward and better treatments.

Mental health, too, is an integral part of preventative care. Building a robust social network, engaging in activities that challenge your mind, and seeking moments of reflection and relaxation can all contribute to a resilient attitude. Emotional health is the support that helps us through tough times; taking care of it is just as important as looking after our physical health.

You may also want to consider the role of supplements and

medications. While not a substitute for a healthy lifestyle, they can be powerful when used correctly and under the guidance of healthcare professionals. They can bolster our defenses, correct imbalances, and support the body's intricate biological systems.

Each day is an opportunity to nurture the pillars of our health. Preventative care is an ongoing journey of small, consistent steps—a daily dose of care accumulating into a lifetime of wellness. By staying ahead of health challenges, we proactively avoid the pitfalls of age and elevate the quality of our years, ensuring each chapter of our lives is lived to the best of our ability.

Preventative care turns into a life approach. It understands that even though we can't control time, we can improve how we live through it. Every careful decision we make strengthens how we live our lives, creating a healthy legacy that can motivate future generations.

Chapter Summary

- Nutrition becomes more critical as we age, requiring a balanced diet rich in nutrients, a focus on nutrient-dense foods and proper hydration to support bodily changes.
- Antioxidants and omega-3 fatty acids are essential for reducing inflammation and supporting heart health.
- Social and emotional aspects of eating contribute to overall well-being, making meals a time for connection.
- Regular exercise is essential for maintaining physical strength, cardiovascular health, and cognitive function.
- Social connections and mental stimulation can help foster resilience and improve our well-being as we age.

- Sleep is vital for physical repair and cognitive function, with changes in sleep patterns common as we get older.
- Preventative care, including a healthy lifestyle, regular check-ups, and mental health maintenance, can help you age more gracefully.

2

RELATIONSHIPS AND SOCIAL CONNECTIONS

Our relationships become ever more precious as we continue our journey through life. The bonds with our family grow deeper, and caring for these relationships becomes a vital part of aging beautifully.

Family ties offer a unique form of support and understanding deeply rooted in shared history and love. These bonds are the foundation upon which we can lean when other aspects of our lives shift. As we age, we may find that roles within the family evolve; parents may become care recipients rather than providers, siblings may become peers in the aging process, and children may take on supportive roles that reverse the dynamics of childhood.

Communication is vital in nurturing these familial relationships. Through open and honest dialogue, we can address the changing needs and expectations that come with aging. It is not uncommon for misunderstandings to arise, as the transition into new roles can be challenging for all involved. However, when approached with empathy and patience, these conversations can strengthen familial bonds, creating a resilient support network.

The sharing of memories and the creation of new ones play a significant role in reinforcing family ties. Whether recounting tales of the past or experiencing new adventures together, storytelling helps connect generations. It is a way to pass on wisdom, share laughter, and keep the essence of who we are alive within the hearts of our loved ones.

In addition to emotional support, families often provide practical assistance to one another. This can range from helping with day-to-day tasks to making important health or financial decisions. Navigate these exchanges with respect for each other's autonomy and dignity. Finding a balance between offering help and allowing independence can be delicate, but it is vital for maintaining a sense of self-worth and mutual respect.

Cultivating close family relationships is both a source of comfort and a powerful contributor to our overall well-being. These connections offer a sense of belonging, a cushion against the challenges of aging, and a reminder that we are part of a continuum that stretches both behind and ahead of us.

The love and care we invest in our family relationships are perhaps the most enduring legacy we can leave. Through these bonds, our influence and memories will persist, providing guidance and strength for future generations. Ultimately, the grace with which we age is reflected in the warmth and resilience of the family bonds we nurture.

Friendship in Later Life: The Value of Companionship

As we move through life, friendships become more valuable, adding warmth and color to our older years. The importance of having friends is huge because it's with them that we share joy, support, and a shared view of our changing world.

In our later years, friendships can change and grow. Friends from our younger days might have been with us through life's ups and downs, seeing our struggles and successes. These lasting bonds are rich with shared memories, giving us comfort that we have someone who remembers the past with us.

It is also a time when new friendships can blossom. Retirement communities, senior centers, and various hobby groups provide an opportunity for new connections. These friendships are built on the common ground of shared experiences of aging, the understanding of loss, and the appreciation of every moment. They are less about where we have been and more about where we are now, in this moment, together.

The companionship of friends in later life is a balm for the soul. It can alleviate the lonely experience that sometimes accompanies the quiet of an empty nest or the loss of a lifelong partner. Friends can offer a listening ear, a hand to hold during a doctor's visit, or a shared joke that ignites laughter, proving that happiness does not diminish with age.

These relationships are vital to our well-being. Studies have shown that social connections can profoundly impact our physical health, from lowering blood pressure to reducing the risk of chronic diseases. They also sharpen our minds, as engaging in conversations and social activities keeps our brains active and resilient.

The art of friendship in later life also involves a delicate balance of giving and receiving. It is about being there for others, just as they are there for you, creating a mutual support system. This exchange fosters a sense of purpose and belonging, reminding you that you are never too old to make a difference in someone else's life.

As we appreciate friendship, we must also acknowledge the challenges that can arise. Losing friends over time or because they're far away can be difficult. But the courage to reach out, make new friends, and cherish the memories of friends past keeps the joy of companionship alive.

As we continue to live, remember the simplicity in a cup of tea shared with a friend, the stories exchanged on a park bench, or the silent understanding that passes between two souls who have experienced life's challenges together. These moments of connection truly define the richness of our later years.

Friendship in our later years is an integral part of aging well. It's about the laughter, the memories we share, and the support we give each other that show us we're all part of the human experience, full of life and forever linked.

Community Engagement: Finding Your Place

After exploring the transformative value of companionship, it's important to recognize another type of social connection essential to aging with grace: community engagement.

Finding your place within a community is similar to discovering a garden where you can continue to grow, blossom, and contribute to the vibrant ecosystem of life. Within this garden, you can find a sense of belonging and the opportunity to cultivate new skills, share wisdom, and experience a renewed sense of purpose.

Community engagement is a broad term covering various activities and roles. It can mean volunteering at local organizations, participating in group activities at senior centers, joining clubs or societies that align with your interests, or even leading initiatives that benefit the wider community. The beauty of community involvement is that it offers a platform for individuals to step outside of themselves and connect with others through shared interests.

There are many benefits of such engagement. Socially, it opens doors to new friendships and strengthens existing ones, creating an invaluable support network as we age. Emotionally, it can boost self-esteem and combat feelings of loneliness or isolation. Intellectually, it challenges the mind through organizing events, learning new skills, or simply engaging in stimulating conversations. Physically, it often encourages activity and movement, which are vital to maintaining health and mobility.

Community engagement also provides a sense of continuity and legacy. It allows older adults to pass on their knowledge and experiences to younger generations, fostering intergenerational connections that enrich both the givers and receivers of this exchange. It's a way to remain active, ensuring your life is filled with meaningful stories and impactful lessons.

Finding your place within a community may take time and require some exploration. It's about identifying what resonates with your passions and values. It could be through art, music, education, or environmental stewardship. It might involve mentoring others, advocating for causes close to your heart, or being a consistent presence in a group that shares your interests.

Getting involved in the community doesn't need to be a big task. Small acts of kindness, like checking in on a neighbor or contributing to a communal garden, are just as impactful. Every little bit helps add to the community's strength and your well-being.

As you embrace community engagement, prepare yourself for new kinds of relationships to blossom. The connections made through shared community activities can sometimes lead to unexpected companionship, proving that the heart, like the spirit of community, knows no age.

Finding your place within the community is about creating a space where you can continue to learn, share, and contribute. It's about creating a sense of belonging that extends to being part of the community and the lives of others. It's a journey that reaffirms life's vibrancy at any age and highlights our lasting ability to grow and connect with others.

Romance After Retirement: Love Knows No Age

Your later years, often seen as a period of winding down, can also be a time of new and unexpected beginnings, including romance. The belief that love is only for the young is overthrown with every story of those who have found new partners in their older years.

Love in old age is a testament to the human desire for connection and intimacy. It enables us to experience companionship to combat loneliness and the joy of sharing life's simple pleasures with someone who understands the value of each passing day. For many, romance at this stage is not a whirlwind of passion but rather a gentle breeze that brings warmth and comfort to the soul.

Finding love later in life often means bringing a wealth of experience into a new relationship. It's about understanding that every person has a past and experiences of joys, sorrows, triumphs, and challenges. These experiences can create new relationships grounded in empathy, patience, and mutual respect that may have been harder to come by in younger years.

For those who have lost a lifelong partner, the idea of romance can be accompanied by guilt and hesitation. But remember that the ability to love does not diminish with age or the loss of a loved one. The heart's capacity to love again honors past love and the potential for future love. It's a courageous move, trusting in the chance for happiness and recognizing that life always offers new chapters.

How people have found love has evolved with the times. Social gatherings, community events, and digital dating platforms are now part of the narrative. The internet has opened doors for those who might not have the opportunity to meet potential partners in their day-to-day lives, allowing for connections beyond geographical boundaries. It's a world where a simple message sent at night could turn into a coffee date and the start of a new life together.

In these relationships, the focus often shifts from the external to the internal. Shared values, interests, and dreams for the future become the glue that binds one to another. It's less about what one can provide materially and more about an emotional and spiritual connection.

As we continue to form new connections in later years, it becomes clear that love, in its many forms, remains an integral part of our human experience. Love knows no age and is a force that not only endures but often grows stronger with time. In the next section, we will delve into the delicate subject of loss and how to find solace and support in times of sorrow.

Dealing with Loss: Finding Strength in Community

The connections we make throughout life, from short-lived acquaintances to deep-rooted friendships, form a network that supports us, brings us joy, and gives our days meaning. However, an inevitable part of this journey is the experience of loss. It is a universal truth that we will face the departure of friends, partners, and loved ones as we age. Through our community, we can find the resilience to embrace these changes with grace and courage.

Loss can often cast a shadow over our spirit. The pain of absence can be overwhelming, and the silence left behind by someone who's gone can feel deafening. But it is important to remember that you are not alone in this. The support network around you, both near and far, is a source of incredible strength. Within this circle of care, we can find solace and a path to healing.

When you experience loss, reaching out may feel like the last thing you want to do, but it is often the first step towards healing. Sharing your stories, memories, and grief can open the door to comfort and understanding from others who have experienced similar things. Support groups, formal or informal, provide a space where emotions can be expressed without judgment and where the burden of sorrow can be shared.

Engaging in community activities can be another remedy for an aching heart. Volunteering, joining clubs, or participating in local events can serve as a distraction and a means to forge new connections and find purpose. These activities can reignite a sense of belonging, reminding us that our presence is valued and that our contributions to the world around us are still needed.

In these moments of vulnerability, the true depth of our relationships is often revealed. Friends and family may come forward in ways we never expected, offering support through listening, helping with daily tasks, or simply being present. Sometimes, the quiet companionship of sitting with someone who understands, without the need for words, can provide the greatest comfort.

As we continue to age, it is essential to cultivate and nurture these social connections. When woven together, they are the threads that create a safety net of emotional support. And when one thread breaks, the strength of the others helps hold us together.

In embracing community, we also learn to accept the changing nature of our relationships. New friendships can blossom in the most unexpected places, and these bonds can be just as meaningful and enriching as those we've held for a lifetime. The key is to remain open—to people, experiences, and the possibility that every encounter can bring something valuable into our lives.

Dealing with loss is never easy, but it is a journey that does not have to be walked alone. By finding strength in community, we can face loss and change with hope and the knowledge that, even amid sorrow, we are surrounded by a network of people ready to hold us up. Aging with grace involves recognizing the beauty and resilience that comes from being part of something greater than ourselves—a community that sustains us through all seasons of life.

Chapter Summary

- As we age, nurturing close family relationships becomes increasingly important for emotional support and well-being. Communication, sharing memories, and providing practical assistance are crucial to maintaining strong family ties in later life.
- Friendships in later years are crucial for laughter, support, and understanding and can improve physical health and cognitive function.
- Community engagement through volunteering, joining clubs, and participating in group activities offers social, emotional, intellectual, and physical benefits.
- Finding new roles and purpose within your community as you age is always possible, contributing to a sense of belonging and legacy.
- Romance after retirement is always possible, with shared values and experiences forming the basis of new

relationships. The internet and social gatherings allow people to meet potential partners and pursue new romantic connections later in life.
- Dealing with loss is a part of aging, but strength can be found in community support, new friendships, and continued engagement in social activities.

3

PERSONAL GROWTH AND LIFELONG LEARNING

The concept of time often changes as we age. Far from the frenetic pace of earlier decades, later years can unfold with a gentler, more reflective pace. This period offers the promise of personal enrichment and the opportunity to embrace new challenges with open arms.

Whether learning a new language, picking up a paintbrush for the first time, or delving into the digital world, each new activity we try demonstrates our ability to grow and adapt.

Consider the story of Harriet, who, at the age of seventy-two, decided to turn her lifelong fascination with pottery into a tangible skill. Despite initial trepidation, she joined a local ceramics class. With each session, her hands became more confident in molding the clay, and her sense of accomplishment grew alongside her skill. Harriet's journey allowed her to redefine her own limits and discover a new mode of self-expression.

Embracing new challenges later in life is also a celebration of courage. It takes bravery to step into the unknown, to be a beginner amongst others who might be decades younger. Yet, this act of courage is incredibly empowering. It sends a clear message: age is not a barrier to learning but rather a platform from which to leap into new experiences.

The pursuit of new challenges has a ripple effect that extends beyond personal fulfillment. It can inspire peers and younger generations, showing them that learning and growth are lifelong journeys. Engaging in something new contributes to a more vibrant, intergenerational exchange of ideas and perspectives, enriching your relationships with your community.

When we embrace these new challenges, we experience a subtle yet significant shift in perspective. Success is no longer measured by the mastery of a task but by the bliss found in the pursuit itself. The focus is on the process, the daily incremental improvements, and the pleasure of engaging with something novel and stimulating.

The next step in this journey is to delve into intellectual curiosity and how keeping the mind sharp is integral to aging with grace.

Intellectual Curiosity: Keeping the Mind Sharp

A love for learning keeps us young and reminds us of the unending energy of our spirit. Much like our body's muscles, the mind thrives on engagement, challenge, and nourishment. It is this intellectual curiosity that helps keep our minds sharp and adaptable.

Embracing a lifestyle of learning and exploration is a commitment to ourselves. It recognizes that our capacity for growth and understanding is not finite but an ever-expanding horizon. The beauty of this pursuit lies in its accessibility; learning does not discriminate against age, and the world is full of knowledge waiting to be discovered.

You could turn to books to keep the mind sharp, which offer a universe of wisdom, stories, and ideas. Reading is a sanctuary, a place where you can engage with the thoughts of others, challenge preconceptions, and build new perspectives. It is an exercise that can be both solitary and communal, as book clubs and discussion groups provide a space for shared discovery and camaraderie.

Beyond the pages of books, the digital age has welcomed an era where learning is more available than ever before. Online courses, lectures, and workshops allow you to delve into subjects that excite your interest, from the arts and sciences to history and philosophy. This democratization of knowledge empowers us to take ownership of our intellectual journeys and tailor our learning experiences to our interests.

Intellectual curiosity often leads to the joy of problem-solving and critical thinking. Engaging in puzzles, strategic games, or learning a new language can offer mental stimulation that is both enjoyable and beneficial. These activities keep the neural pathways active, encouraging the brain to form new connections and maintain its plasticity.

In this quest for knowledge, celebrate every new thing you

understand, knowing that each detail you learn and each idea you grasp is a triumph against the dullness that can often come with aging. In these moments of insight, we often find a profound sense of accomplishment and purpose.

A love for learning goes hand in hand with creativity, guiding us to new ways to express ourselves and find satisfaction. The arts welcome us, providing a way to use our curiosity to keep our minds and lives filled with knowledge and creativity.

Creative Expression: The Arts as a Lifeline

Personal growth and learning often go hand in hand in the arts. Creative expression is more than just a hobby; it's an essential connection to our inner being, other people, and the wider world.

The arts offer a unique form of communication that transcends age, language, and culture barriers. Whether through painting, music, writing, or dance, engaging in creative activities can provide a sense of purpose and a channel for expressing hidden emotions. For many, creation is a deeply therapeutic process, allowing them to release feelings and explore new perspectives.

The beauty of the arts lies in their accessibility; you don't need to be a professional artist to reap the benefits. Community centers, local colleges, and other organizations offer classes and workshops for all ages, encouraging you to explore your creativity in a supportive environment.

The arts can also serve as a bridge to connect generations. Grandparents can share stories through written memoirs or oral histories, imparting wisdom and preserving family legacies. Collaborative projects, such as quilting or community theater, foster social connections and a sense of belonging, essential for well-being at any age.

There are also cognitive benefits of engaging with the arts.

Learning to play a musical instrument, for example, can enhance memory, sharpen concentration, and improve hand-eye coordination. Similarly, the visual-spatial skills required for drawing or sculpting can help maintain mental awareness.

But perhaps the most profound impact of the arts is the way they allow for continuous self-discovery. Each brushstroke, note, and word written allows you to explore new facets of your identity. The arts remind us that growth does not cease with age; instead, it becomes a deeper and more thoughtful journey.

The arts become a source of joy and rejuvenation in embracing creative expression. They encourage us to remain curious, play, experiment, and view each day as a canvas awaiting our unique creations. Through the arts, we learn that aging with grace can be done by creating new experiences that enrich our lives and the lives of those around us.

The arts can also prepare our minds for the more profound questions and reflections that come with contemplating life's profound journey.

Spirituality and Aging: Seeking Meaning

As we age, many people look inside themselves for deeper meaning and spiritual satisfaction. This search for spiritual insight isn't just an escape from life's complexities but a deep connection with the core of what it means to be alive.

Spirituality is a connection to something greater than oneself. It can be found through religion, personal belief systems, nature, or the connections we forge with others. Spirituality often becomes more significant as we age, serving as a source of comfort, strength, and guiding light.

The search for meaning in later life is a pursuit that can lead to personal growth. It is about asking the big questions: Who am I?

Why am I here? What legacy will I leave behind? These questions invigorate the spirit, offering a chance for reflection and self-discovery.

For some, spirituality may involve rekindling faith or a newfound interest in religious practices. Places of worship not only provide a sense of community but also opportunities for service and the sharing of life's milestones. For others, spirituality may manifest in meditation, the practice of mindfulness, or the simple act of being present in the moment. These practices can help to still the mind, soothe the soul, and provide clarity amidst life's uncertainties.

Spirituality also can be a source of resilience. It can help individuals cope with loss—whether it be the loss of loved ones, the loss of physical abilities, or the changing dynamics of social circles. It offers a framework to understand and accept these changes, providing a sense of peace and the ability to let go with grace.

In embracing spirituality, we also embrace life as a continuous learning journey. We learn to remain open to new experiences, ideas, and perspectives. This openness can lead to a deeper appreciation for the interconnectedness of all things and the recognition that our lives are part of a larger narrative.

Cultivating spiritual well-being is not about finding definitive answers to life's mysteries. Instead, it is about living in the questions, embracing the unknown, and finding thrill in the search itself. It is about understanding that every moment is precious and that our spirits can continue to soar unbounded by age.

This process of self-discovery leads us to the next contemplation: the importance of legacy and storytelling. Here, we explore how spiritual insights and personal growth gained in our later years can be passed down, enriching the lives of others and ensuring that our stories echo into the future.

Legacy and Storytelling: Passing on Wisdom

Storytelling is as ancient as humanity itself, and the stories we share become the vessels of our wisdom and the legacy we leave behind for future generations.

Storytelling is not simply about recounting events; it is about imparting the lessons we have learned, the values we cherish, and the insights we have gained. It is an enriching way to connect with others and bridge the gap between generations and cultures. As we age gracefully, we become the custodians of our family's history and the guardians of its future.

When we share our stories, we offer a roadmap to those who walk the paths we once tread. We reveal the decisions that shaped our lives, the moments that tested our resolve, and the love that sustained us. Our narratives become a source of comfort and inspiration, encouraging resilience and fostering understanding in those who listen.

The wisdom we pass on is not always found in spectacular tales; often, it is nestled in the simplest of anecdotes. It could be the story of a particular holiday meal that taught us the importance of family or a recollection of a chance encounter that changed our perspective on life. These stories are the gifts we give, timeless and more precious than any material possession.

Storytelling is a reciprocal process. As we share, we also invite others to share with us, creating a dialogue that honors the collective wisdom of our community. This exchange nurtures a sense of belonging and continuity, reinforcing that while we are unique, we are all part of a larger human narrative.

In embracing our role as storytellers, we must also be mindful of how we craft our legacies. It is not enough to speak; strive to speak with intention, hoping our words will empower and uplift. We must be honest yet kind, reflective yet forward-looking. Our stories should not be educational lectures but open offerings encouraging others to reflect, dream, and grow.

As you consider the stories you wish to pass on, consider how you share them. In an age where technology allows for our voices to be heard far and wide, we can leave a lasting imprint on those immediately around us and the world at large. Whether through written memoirs, recorded interviews, or casual conversations around the dinner table, our stories have the power to transcend time and space.

The wisdom we share through our stories guides the young and reassures the old that their journey has meaning. As we age gracefully, take comfort in knowing that we continue contributing to the world's dialogue long after our final bow through our stories.

Chapter Summary

- Embracing new challenges shows our commitment to personal growth and our lasting ability to learn and adjust.
- Pursuing new endeavors, such as learning new skills or hobbies, is empowering and demonstrates that age is not a barrier to learning.
- Engaging in lifelong learning inspires others, enriches communities, and focuses on the joy of the pursuit rather than just mastery.
- Intellectual curiosity keeps the mind sharp and can help us age gracefully.
- Creative expression through the arts offers therapeutic benefits, cognitive enhancement, and opportunities for self-discovery and intergenerational connection.

- Spirituality may gain importance later in life, providing comfort, strength, and a means to seek deeper meaning and cope with life's changes.
- Storytelling is a powerful tool for passing on wisdom and connecting generations with personal narratives, offering comfort and inspiration.
- Legacy is crafted through intentional storytelling, with technology allowing for a broader impact and ensuring that personal stories and wisdom echo into the future.

4

FINANCIAL SECURITY AND PLANNING

Managing money can feel more challenging as we enter our later years, with income and costs changing unexpectedly. During this time, budgeting becomes a practical skill and a way to create a secure and peaceful life after retirement.

Budgeting, in its essence, is about balance. It balances our resources and the life we want to lead. As we age, this balance must be struck with an awareness of the changing rhythms of life. The budget that served us well in our earlier years may no longer fit the quieter, perhaps slower, tempo of our golden years.

First, take a compassionate and realistic look at your income sources. These may include social security, pensions, retirement accounts, investments, and part-time work. Understanding your income flow allows you to plan your activities and spending accordingly.

Next, consider your expenses. Some costs may decrease as you age, such as work-related expenses or mortgage payments if your home is paid off. However, other costs, like healthcare and long-term care, can rise, sometimes unexpectedly. It's important to budget for what you know and set aside funds for unforeseen events that may try to unsettle your financial plan.

One of the most empathetic steps you can take is to ensure that your budget includes room for the things that bring joy and fulfillment. Whether it's a hobby, travel, or contributions to things that are important to you, these are the expenditures that breathe life into your years and should not be neglected.

In managing your budget, spreadsheets or budgeting software can be invaluable tools. They allow you to visualize your financial landscape, track your spending, and adjust as needed. Remember, a budget is not set in stone; it is a living document that should evolve as your needs and circumstances change.

As you refine your budget, consider the legacy you wish to leave. This may involve estate planning, gifting to loved ones, or charity donations. These decisions, too, should be incorporated into your financial plan, ensuring that your values extend beyond your own journey.

Budgeting for later life goes beyond just tracking numbers; it's about shaping your life's story so that your finances support the life you want to lead. It's navigating life's changes gracefully, planning wisely for tough times, and having the courage to enjoy the good times.

As you work through the practicalities of budgeting, you might start considering the next chapter of your financial journey—investing in retirement. Here, the goal changes from keeping daily peace to staying stable despite economic shifts. With a well-considered budget, you can explore strategies to help ensure your financial security so you can age with the grace and freedom you deserve.

Investing in Retirement: Strategies for Stability

As we enter retirement, financial planning gets more complex. Investing at this stage isn't about getting rich but about creating a steady flow of income that supports a happy and satisfying life.

Investing during retirement is significantly different from the growth-focused strategies of earlier years. It's a time when the focus shifts from wealth accumulation to wealth preservation and income generation. Your strategies must be tailored to your circumstances, including your health, life expectancy, and the legacy you wish to leave behind.

One of the cornerstones of a stable retirement investment strategy is diversification. Diversification is the financial equivalent of not putting all your eggs in one basket. It involves spreading investments across various asset classes, such as stocks, bonds, real estate, and possibly annuities, to mitigate risk. While stocks may offer growth potential and combat inflation over the long term, bonds can provide a more stable and predictable income. Real estate investments can offer both income through rental yields and potential appreciation in value. On the other hand, annuities can offer a guaranteed income for life, which can be a comforting thought for many retirees.

Another strategy to consider is the careful use of the bucket approach. This involves dividing your investments into "buckets" based on when you will need to access the funds. The first bucket, for instance, could contain cash and cash equivalents for immediate needs. The second bucket might include short-term fixed-income investments you'll need in the next few years. The third bucket, aimed at the long-term, could be more growth-oriented, containing stocks and real estate investments you won't need to touch for several years. This approach ensures that you have funds available when needed while still allowing for growth potential.

The concept of asset allocation also remains critical during retirement. It's about finding the right balance between different types of investments to align with your risk tolerance and time horizon. Our risk tolerance typically decreases as we age, and our investment horizon shortens. Therefore, a shift towards more conservative investments may be needed. However, with increasing life expectancies, it's also important to maintain some growth-oriented investments to ensure our assets last as long as we do.

It's also essential to be mindful of the impact of inflation on fixed incomes. Even at low rates, inflation can significantly erode purchasing power over time. Investments that have the potential to outpace inflation, such as certain stocks or real estate, can be important components of your portfolio as you grow older.

Tax efficiency is another concept to be aware of in retirement. Understanding which accounts to withdraw from first and how to organize your assets for maximum efficiency can substantially affect how long your savings last. Investing strategies like focusing on long-term capital gains and qualified dividends can help stretch your retirement dollars.

Take time to review and adjust your investment strategy regularly. Life changes, market conditions shift, and personal needs evolve. An annual review of your financial plan with a trusted advisor can ensure that your investment strategy continues to align with your current situation and goals.

Investing in retirement is not about chasing returns but creating a harmonious balance, supporting your lifestyle, and bringing peace of mind. It's about ensuring that your financial resources align with your life and the legacy you wish to create. With careful planning and thoughtful strategy, you can navigate the financial currents of retirement with confidence and grace.

Navigating Pensions and Social Security

Our financial situation shifts in significant ways as we age. We move from earning money to depending on what we've saved and planned for, like pensions and Social Security. Managing these funds isn't just for financial stability; it's a way to respect our work and the life we've created.

Pensions, once the foundation of retirement security, have become less common in the private sector. Yet, they remain a significant source of income for many retirees. If you are fortunate to have a pension, it's essential to comprehend the different payout options available to you. Some pensions offer a lump-sum payment, while others provide a guaranteed monthly benefit. Each choice impacts your financial longevity differently and can affect your loved ones after you're gone. It's a decision that requires careful consideration, and often, the counsel of a financial advisor can help illuminate the path that best aligns with your circumstances and goals.

Social Security, a program that has been a safety net for countless Americans, is a more universal aspect of retirement planning. Deciding when to start taking Social Security benefits is a pivotal choice that requires a thoughtful strategy. The decision of when to claim should be made with an eye on your health, financial needs, and employment status, among other factors.

If you're married, divorced, or widowed, additional considerations must be considered. Spousal benefits, survivor benefits, and the implications of marriage duration on your entitlements can all influence your Social Security strategy. These rules can be complex, and navigating them is often akin to learning a new language late in life. Yet, understanding them is crucial to maximizing the benefits you've earned.

In managing pensions and Social Security, it's essential to consider how these income streams interact with your overall retirement plan. They can impact your tax situation, how you draw down other retirement savings, and even your healthcare choices. It's a delicate balancing act that benefits from ongoing review as policies and personal circumstances evolve.

Estate Planning: Preparing for the Future

As we grow older, our lives become filled with memories and experiences, and we start to think about the legacy we want to leave. Estate planning is crucial to financial security, and a deep act of love for our family and the things we care about. Careful planning for the future ensures our wishes are respected, and our loved ones are cared for.

Estate planning can be a delicate journey because it requires us to confront our mortality with courage and clarity. It is a process that involves organizing our financial affairs and making decisions that will have lasting impacts. To begin, one must take stock of all assets, including property, investments, and personal possessions of sentimental value. This comprehensive inventory is the foundation upon which your estate plan is built.

A will is often the most important part of an estate plan. It is a legal document that outlines your desires about distributing your assets and caring for any minor children. Without a will, these decisions typically fall to the state, which may not align with your wishes. Therefore, drafting a will with the assistance of a legal professional is an essential step.

In addition to a will, there are other instruments and strategies to consider. Trusts can be established to manage your assets according to your directives, potentially offering tax benefits and protection from legal challenges. Powers of attorney and healthcare directives are also vital, as they designate individuals to make financial and medical decisions on your behalf if you cannot do so.

It is also important to consider the potential impact of taxes on your estate. Thoughtful planning can help minimize the tax burden on those you leave behind, preserving more of your legacy for their benefit. Charitable giving can be part of this strategy, allowing you to support the causes that are important to you while also providing tax advantages.

Estate planning is not a one-time task but an evolving process. Life's changes—such as marriage, divorce, the birth of a child, or the acquisition of significant assets—may require you to update your plan. Regular reviews with your attorney and financial advisor can help ensure your estate plan continues to reflect your current circumstances and wishes.

So far, we have explored the practical steps of estate planning, but let's not forget the emotional and relational aspects. Communicating with your loved ones about your plans can prevent misunderstandings and ensure clear intentions. It can also provide an opportunity for meaningful conversations about values, memories, and the hopes you have for your family's future.

Estate planning is an act of foresight and compassion. It is a way to honor your life and express your love and care for those you will one day leave behind. By preparing for the future, you can offer your loved ones the gift of security and peace of mind, knowing that your legacy will be preserved according to your deepest wishes.

The Role of Insurance in Protecting Your Legacy

The idea of legacy becomes more prominent and meaningful during our later years. It becomes more about the impact we make and the safety we ensure for our loved ones rather than the money we've gathered. Insurance is crucial in financial security and planning, tied to our wish to safeguard and continue our legacy for those who come after us.

Insurance acts as a protection against unexpected events. It shows we've planned carefully to ensure our loved ones won't face financial trouble when we're gone. Life insurance is especially important in this protective plan.

Think of life insurance as a quiet vow, a pledge that lasts even after we're gone. It's a promise that if our passing could shake our family's financial security, they will have a safety net. The money from a life insurance policy can help maintain stability during tough times, helping to pay off debts, cover everyday costs, and support dreams like education or buying a home.

However, the role of insurance in protecting your legacy extends beyond life insurance. Long-term care insurance, for example, addresses the reality that with age comes the potential need for assistance with daily living activities. This type of insurance can alleviate the financial strain of long-term care, preserving your estate's assets and ensuring that the wealth you intended to pass on remains intact.

Similarly, disability insurance plays a pivotal role for those still in their working years. It's a hedge against the possibility that an illness or injury could interrupt your ability to earn an income.

This type of insurance similarly helps maintain your standard of living. It safeguards your savings, allowing you to continue contributing to your legacy without the added stress of financial hardship.

Property and casualty insurance protects the tangible assets you've worked hard to acquire. Homeowners insurance, auto insurance, and umbrella policies protect against the financial repercussions of accidents, natural disasters, and unforeseen events that could otherwise deplete your estate.

Each insurance policy should be a strategic piece of your broader legacy plan. It's about ensuring that the values you've lived by—responsibility, protection, and care—are upheld even when you're no longer there to champion them yourself.

Insurance is about protecting your family from the financial unknowns of life and death. When considering the legacy you want to leave, consider how insurance can be a reliable support in your journey to age with grace and dignity, ensuring you leave behind a legacy of lasting stability and peace of mind, not a burden.

Chapter Summary

- Budgeting in later years is crucial for balancing income and expenses, and one must adapt their financial plans to the slower pace of retirement.
- Income sources like social security, pensions, and investments must be understood, and expenses, including rising healthcare costs, should be carefully considered.
- Budgeting for joy and fulfillment through hobbies, travel, or donations is essential, using tools like spreadsheets or software for tracking.

- Estate planning and considering the legacy you wish to leave should be part of financial planning.
- Retirement investment strategies should focus on stability and income generation, with diversification across asset classes.
- Regularly reviewing and adjusting investment strategies is essential to align with life changes and market conditions.
- Understanding pensions and Social Security benefits is important in retirement, including when to claim benefits and how they affect overall financial planning.
- Estate planning involves creating a will, setting up trusts, and ensuring one's wishes are honored, with regular updates as circumstances change.

5

THE ART OF ADAPTATION: EMBRACING CHANGE

Our bodies, like the seasons, undergo their own transformations as we journey through life. Aging with grace requires us to understand and accept these physical changes. It is a natural part of life that reflects the lives we've lived and the experiences we've valued. However, embracing this new phase can be as challenging as it is inevitable.

Everyone experiences physical change in different ways. Some may notice a difference in strength and stamina, while others may observe changes in skin texture or hair color. Our vision and hearing might not be as sharp as they once were, and we may find ourselves adjusting the font size on our devices or asking others to speak up a bit more often.

Recognizing and accepting these changes does not mean resignation. It means acknowledging the natural course of life and adapting our lifestyles to maintain our health and well-being. It's about finding new ways to stay active that accommodate our changing bodies. Perhaps the long runs of our youth transition into brisk walks or gentle yoga sessions. It's about nourishing our bodies with the right foods, rich in nutrients, that support our vitality at every age.

Understanding our physical changes involves a compassionate dialogue with ourselves. It's about looking in the mirror and seeing beyond the lines and gray hairs to the wisdom and stories they represent. It's about celebrating the body that has allowed us to experience the world in its full splendor and continues to do so, albeit at a different pace.

In this acceptance, there is a quiet strength. It's the strength to ask for help when simple tasks become challenging and the courage to adapt our environments to our needs—through assistive devices or home modifications. It's the strength to share our vulnerabilities with loved ones, fostering deeper connections and mutual support.

Adapting to our physical changes, we pave the way for mental adaptability. Staying flexible in our thoughts and attitudes becomes just as important as maintaining flexibility in our joints. The grace with which we accept our physical selves feeds into the resilience of our minds, allowing us to approach each new day with curiosity and openness.

In the next steps of our journey, we will explore the mental landscape of aging, understanding that our thoughts and attitudes can either be our greatest allies or our most challenging obstacles. As we adapt physically, let us also prepare to cultivate mental adaptability, embracing the full spectrum of changes that come with time.

Mental Adaptability: Staying Flexible

Let's now explore the landscape of the mind, where adaptability and flexibility become our allies in the art of aging with grace.

Mental adaptability is embracing change with an open heart and an agile mind. It is about cultivating a mindset that welcomes transformation as a natural part of life. As we age, our cognitive processes may shift, and our perspectives may evolve, but this does not signify an end to growth. Instead, it presents an opportunity for new learning and different ways of engaging with the world.

We must challenge ourselves to remain curious and open to new ideas to stay mentally flexible. It can be as simple as taking up a new hobby, learning a new language, or engaging in regular intellectual discussions with friends or family. These activities stimulate the brain, fostering neural plasticity, the brain's remarkable ability to reorganize itself by forming new neural connections throughout life.

Another aspect of mental adaptability is the practice of mindfulness. Mindfulness encourages us to live in the present moment and to observe our thoughts and feelings without judgment. This practice can help us navigate the emotional landscape of aging, allowing us to acknowledge and accept our feelings of loss, joy, or anything in between. By being present, we can appreciate the richness of each moment, even as we acknowledge the changes that come with time.

Resilience, too, plays a pivotal role in mental adaptability. Life can sometimes present challenges that test our emotional and psychological limits. As we explored in earlier chapters, building resilience involves developing coping strategies that help us bounce back from adversity. It is about finding strength in vulnerability and learning that it is okay to ask for help when needed. Support networks, whether they consist of family, friends, or community resources, can provide the encouragement and assistance necessary to navigate life's more turbulent waters.

Mental flexibility requires accepting change and embracing it with wisdom and courage. It is about understanding that each new chapter of life brings the potential for growth, discovery, and a deeper appreciation for the mosaic of experiences that define our unique journey through the years.

We must also consider the spaces we inhabit. Our environment plays a significant role in our well-being. As such, the next focus of our journey will be on how we can adjust our living spaces to cater to our changing needs and desires. By harmonizing our external surroundings with our internal states, we create a sanctuary that accommodates our physical requirements and nourishes our mental and emotional health.

Home and Environment: Adjusting Your Living Space

Our homes are often more than just physical spaces; they are repositories of memories, comfort, and personal expression. However, as we age, we may need to reconsider the suitability of our living spaces. The art of adaptation is not only about adjusting our mindset but also about ensuring our environments continue to support our evolving needs.

Changing your living space is a way to take care of yourself. It means recognizing the changes in our lives and taking steps to meet those new needs. This can be both liberating and daunting, but it's an important step towards aging gracefully and keeping your independence.

Firstly, consider the layout of your home. Does it support your current lifestyle and mobility? You might find that rearranging furniture to create wider walkways can make navigation easier. Creating a single-level living space can be ideal, but if that's not possible, ensuring that essential facilities, like a bathroom and a space to sleep, are accessible without having to navigate stairs can be a practical compromise.

Floors should be a focus as well. Slip-resistant flooring can safeguard against falls, a leading cause of injury for older adults. Removing or securing rugs with non-slip pads and choosing carpets with a low pile can also help prevent trips and slips.

It's also worth considering the accessibility of everyday items. Placing frequently used objects within easy reach can minimize strain and the need for unnecessary stretching or bending.

Lighting also plays a crucial role in a comfortable living environment. As our eyes age, we may need more light to see clearly. Assess the lighting in your home, and consider adding brighter bulbs and additional light sources where necessary, especially in areas like stairways and hallways where good visibility is crucial.

In the bathroom, where water and hard surfaces pose a significant risk, installing grab bars by the toilet and shower can provide stability and support. A shower seat and a hand-held showerhead can add comfort and reduce the need to stand for prolonged periods. For some, transitioning to a walk-in bathtub or a zero-threshold shower can be a game-changer, blending accessibility with elegance.

In the kitchen, adjusting the height of counters and sinks to accommodate seated use and ensuring that appliances are easily accessible can make daily tasks easier. Lever-style faucet handles and D-shaped cabinet pulls can simplify cooking and cleaning for those with limited hand strength or dexterity.

Staircases, too, can be made safer with sturdy handrails on both sides and a stairlift if navigating the stairs becomes a challenge. Simple organizational changes, like keeping frequently used items within easy reach, can make a significant difference in daily living.

Our emotional connection to specific items or furniture arrangements may make change difficult. However, the goal is to create a space that is not only safe and functional but also one that continues to feel like home. This might mean finding new ways to display cherished mementos or repurposing rooms to suit your hobbies and activities better.

In making these adjustments, involving family, friends, or a professional specializing in age-friendly home design is beneficial. They can offer insights and help execute changes that align with your vision for a comfortable, accessible living space.

Remember, modifying your home is not about erasing the past or admitting your limitations; it's about shaping your environment to fit the vibrant life you continue to lead. It's proof of your adaptability and a pledge to your health as you face the future with hope and elegance.

As we move forward, it's equally important to stay connected with the evolving world around us. The next step in our adaptation journey involves technology, which, when embraced, can enhance our quality of life and keep us engaged with the world.

Technology: Keeping Up with the Times

The fast speed of tech changes can often seem overwhelming. However, getting comfortable with technology can lead to more freedom and a better connection with the world. Learning to use technology is an art of adjusting that can be achieved with patience and willingness to learn.

The digital age has brought about changes that can be both empowering and overwhelming. The key is to approach technology as a tool, not a barrier. It is a means to stay informed, connected, and engaged with our loved ones and the community.

Learning to use new devices and platforms can feel like learning a new language. Still, it's a language that enables us to share stories, view pictures of our grandchildren, and even manage our health. Video calls can shrink the miles between us and our families, and smart devices can remind us to take medication or track our steps for a healthier lifestyle.

Keeping up with technology does not mean chasing every new gadget or trend. Instead, it's about identifying the technologies that add value to our lives. Whether it's a smartphone that helps us stay in touch, a tablet for reading and games, or a home assistant that makes daily tasks easier, each device should serve a purpose that resonates with your needs and interests.

For those who might feel hesitant, remember that learning is a process. Numerous resources, from community classes to online tutorials, cater to all levels of expertise. Family members and friends can also help you on this journey, offering support and companionship as you explore the digital landscape together.

Technology can also offer a sense of safety and security. With medical alert systems and GPS tracking, we can have the peace of mind that help is available at the push of a button. Smart home technologies can automate lighting, heating, and security, ensuring our environment adapts to our needs without requiring constant attention.

As we integrate technology into our lives, remember to maintain a balance. It should never replace the warmth of human contact or the joy of real-world experiences. Instead, let technology enhance how we live, bringing convenience and connection, but always in harmony with the simple pleasures we've always cherished.

In this art of adaptation, we find that when approached with curiosity and a willingness to learn, technology can be a faithful companion on the journey of aging with grace. It allows us to keep up with the times while holding onto the essence of what makes each moment precious.

The Power of Routine: Finding Comfort in Consistency

With age comes a profound beauty in the regularity of daily routines. These routines stitch together the pattern of our everyday life, giving us a comforting structure as we face the natural changes of aging. They're like familiar tunes that provide a rhythm to our changing lives, allowing our days to move smoothly and gracefully.

Over time, routines often become cherished rituals that allow us to maintain a sense of self and purpose. In the quiet moments of morning tea or the evening stroll, their rhythm resonates with our past, present, and future heartbeats.

The strength of routine is that it both anchors and frees us. It gives us a stable structure in life's sea of uncertainties. This isn't about being inflexible; it's about having a framework that brings peace and steadiness. It's like a comforting hand on our shoulder, reminding us that some things stay the same, even as everything else changes.

At the same time, routines liberate us. They free up mental space by reducing the decisions we need to make, allowing us to conserve our energy for the things that truly matter. This is especially poignant in our later years, when we may wish to focus on nurturing relationships, exploring new hobbies, or simply savoring the quiet beauty of the world around us.

However, routines are not set in stone; they are adaptable. As our needs and circumstances change, so too can our routines. This adaptability is key to aging with grace. It is about finding the balance between the comfort of the familiar and the thrill of the new.

In embracing the power of routine, we also embrace the power of self-care. Each step in our daily routine can be an act of kindness towards ourselves. From the nourishing meals we prepare to the restorative sleep we prioritize, each element of our routine is a building block in the temple of our well-being.

Don't underestimate the profound simplicity of a daily routine. They protect our days and care for our well-being quietly. In the art of aging, we should cherish them, as they are the faithful companions that walk alongside us through life's ever-changing seasons.

Chapter Summary

- Aging gracefully involves understanding and accepting the physical changes that come with time, such as decreased strength and changes in vision and hearing.
- Adapting to these changes means finding new ways to stay active, eating nutritious foods, and having a compassionate dialogue with oneself.
- Mental adaptability is crucial as we age, involving staying curious, learning new things, practicing mindfulness, and building resilience.
- Adjusting living spaces to accommodate aging is a form of self-care that may involve changes to your home layout, lighting, and assistive devices.

- Embracing technology can enhance independence and connection with others, and it's important to find a balance and choose technologies that add value.
- Routines provide a comforting sense of order and familiarity, helping to conserve energy for what matters most. They can be adapted to changing needs and circumstances, allowing for both stability and the incorporation of new experiences.
- Daily routines are acts of self-care and can be essential for maintaining well-being as we age.

6

SELF-CARE AND INDEPENDENCE

As we age, the value of daily self-care becomes clearer. It's essential for maintaining our physical health, emotional wellness, and independence. Self-care isn't a luxury; it's a vital set of practices that help us age gracefully and with dignity.

At the heart of daily self-care is personal hygiene. This covers a range of activities from bathing to oral care, each playing a vital role in fostering a sense of self-respect and confidence. Regular bathing refreshes the body, stimulates circulation, and provides a time for self-reflection and relaxation. On the other hand, oral care is crucial for preventing discomfort and maintaining the ability to enjoy a variety of foods.

Nutrition is another form of self-care. As we age, our bodies' needs change, and so must our diets. As we learned in earlier chapters, prioritizing nutrient-dense foods, staying hydrated, and being mindful of portion sizes help maintain energy levels and support bodily functions. It's also about the dining experience, which should be pleasurable and, when possible, a social activity that connects us with others.

Physical activity, tailored to individual ability and preference, is another non-negotiable aspect of self-care. Whether it's a gentle walk, a series of stretches, or a yoga class, regular movement is essential for preserving flexibility, strength, and balance. It also has profound effects on mental health, helping to alleviate stress and promote a positive mood.

Rest is equally important. Quality sleep is restorative, helping to repair the body and consolidate memories. Establishing a regular sleep routine, creating a comfortable sleeping environment, and promptly addressing any sleep disturbances with a healthcare provider are all critical steps in ensuring that rest is a rejuvenating part of daily life.

Mental and emotional care is as important as physical care. Engaging in activities that stimulate the mind, such as reading, puzzles, or learning new skills, helps to keep the brain active and resilient. Equally important is nurturing emotional health by maintaining social connections, seeking laughter and joy, and finding ways to express feelings and thoughts through conversation, writing, or other creative outlets.

Self-care also includes managing health care. This means being proactive about medical appointments, understanding and adhering to prescribed treatments, and maintaining open communication with healthcare providers. It involves being informed and making decisions that align with your values and quality of life.

In embracing these non-negotiables of daily self-care, we honor our present selves and lay the framework for continued independence and quality of life as we age. These daily acts of self-care can help us navigate the changes of aging with more resilience and grace.

Mobility and Accessibility: Tools for Independence

Our needs for getting around and accessing things may evolve over time. This natural change requires us to adapt, not to give up our independence. With the right aids and environmental changes, we can keep moving through our daily lives confidently and independently.

Mobility aids can be a key to maintaining freedom. A well-chosen walking stick can be a trusted companion on strolls, providing stability and reducing the load on weary joints. For those who find greater comfort in additional support, walkers or rollators offer a sturdy frame to lean on, often equipped with seats and baskets that invite rest and carry personal items during outings.

For longer distances or when energy reserves are low, wheelchairs or mobility scooters can be helpful modes of transport. These tools empower us to participate in family gatherings, community events, and outdoor adventures without worrying about tiredness. If you are considering investing in one of these, select a model that aligns with your lifestyle, ensuring it is comfortable and capable of navigating the spaces you frequently wander.

Adapting our homes is equally crucial in fostering independence. Ramps can replace steps, creating smooth transitions from outdoors to indoors. Doorways may be widened to accommodate mobility aids, and thresholds can be minimized to prevent tripping hazards. Smart home devices enable us to control lighting and temperature and even lock doors with the sound of our voice or the touch of a button. These advancements bring peace of mind and reduce the physical strain of household tasks.

Adopting these tools does not diminish our capabilities but rather enhances them. They are not markers of limitations but symbols of our resourcefulness and determination to live on our terms. By embracing mobility and accessibility tools, we make a conscious choice to age with grace, ensuring that our environment adapts to us as much as we adapt.

Personal Safety: Feeling Secure in Your Environment

During this time, our homes become increasingly important as places of comfort and security. The walls that have seen years of emotions and experiences now protect our daily tranquility and safety. Personal safety, often forgotten, is a key part of self-care and keeping our independence as we grow older.

Feeling secure in your environment is not just about locks on the doors or the brightness of outdoor lights; it's about creating a living space that respects your needs and anticipates potential risks. It's about fostering a sense of well-being from knowing you are protected and prepared for the unexpected.

Technology can be a helpful ally in personal safety. Emergency response systems can be worn as pendants or watches, providing a direct line to assistance should you need it. These devices are designed to be unobtrusive and empowering, giving you and your loved ones peace of mind.

But personal safety extends beyond the physical. It's also about feeling secure knowing you have a support network. This network could include family, friends, neighbors, or community services aware of your routines and ready to offer help if your pattern changes unexpectedly. Regular check-ins can be arranged, not as a sign of frailty, but as a proactive approach to staying connected and secure.

In addition to a support network, consider the role of local authorities and community resources. Familiarize yourself with their services, such as neighborhood watch programs or senior safety initiatives. These resources can provide valuable information and assistance, reinforcing the safety net around you.

Lastly, personal safety is deeply intertwined with emotional well-being. A home that feels secure is a space where stress is minimized and relaxation is invited. It's a place where you can move freely, without fear, and sleep soundly, knowing that you have taken steps to ensure your safety and independence.

By integrating these strategies into your daily life, you create not just a house but a home that supports and protects you through the years.

Managing Medications: A Guide to Responsible Use

In our golden years, taking care of ourselves often involves managing different medications, each with its role and significance. Using these medications responsibly is crucial for keeping our health and independence. It's a careful balance that needs focus, good management, and, sometimes, a bit of wisdom.

Understanding the medications you are prescribed is fundamental. Each medication has a role to play in your well-being, and being informed about their effects, side effects, why you're taking them and how they interact with each other is vital. Do not hesitate to ask your healthcare provider questions about your medications. They can give you the knowledge to take your medications safely and effectively.

Organization is your friend when it comes to managing medications. A pill organizer can be a simple yet effective tool, helping track what needs to be taken and when. Some organizers come with compartments for different times of the day, which can be particularly helpful if your medication regimen is complex. Maintaining a medication list that includes dosages, times, and special instructions can be invaluable, especially if you need to visit a healthcare provider unfamiliar with your medical history.

Adherence to your medication schedule is as important as the medications themselves. Missing doses or taking them at the wrong time can diminish their effectiveness and potentially put your health at risk. If you find remembering to take your medications challenging, consider setting alarms on a clock, watch, or smartphone. There are also apps designed to help manage medication schedules, providing reminders and tracking your adherence over time.

Monitoring for side effects is another aspect of responsible medication management. While medications are intended to help you, they can sometimes cause adverse reactions. Be vigilant about any changes in how you feel after starting a new medication or changing a dose. If you notice anything unusual, report it to your healthcare provider promptly. They can determine if what you are experiencing is expected or adjustments must be made.

Lastly, regular reviews of your medications with your healthcare provider are essential. As your body changes with age, so can how it responds to medications. A once-suitable medication may become less so over time, or new options may be available that could work better for you. These reviews are also an opportunity to check that all of your medications are still necessary and to eliminate any that are not, reducing the risk of polypharmacy.

As you continue to curate the narrative of your life, remember that asking for help when needed is not a sign of weakness but rather a wise acknowledgment of the complexity of self-care.

Asking for Help: Balancing Independence and Support

Taking care of ourselves often means balancing staying independent and knowing when to ask for help. This balance changes as our abilities and situations change. As we grow older, it's essential to understand that seeking help isn't a weakness but a sign of strength and wisdom.

Independence is a cherished value that provides a sense of control, dignity, and purpose. It's understandable to cling to it tightly, as it forms a core part of our identity. However, life's natural progression may lead to moments when self-sufficiency becomes challenging. This is where interdependence may be required—a concept that allows for giving and receiving support to benefit all involved.

To ask for help is to engage in an act of self-care. It requires courage to admit that we cannot do everything alone, and it opens up opportunities for growth and connection. When we allow others to assist us, we not only ease our burdens but also enrich the lives of those who step in to lend a hand.

It's essential to recognize the signs that indicate it might be time to seek assistance. Perhaps managing the household has become more taxing, or personal care routines are not as effortless as they once were. Maybe the complexities of managing medications, as discussed earlier, have highlighted the need for a more structured support system. Whatever the indicators, it's important to assess them honestly and take proactive steps.

One of the most practical approaches to asking for help is understanding your needs clearly. Identifying specific tasks requiring assistance can make the process less overwhelming and more manageable. Communicating openly with loved ones about these needs is beneficial, as they may not always be apparent to others.

When reaching out for help, consider the various resources available. Family and friends are often the first line of support, but there are also community services, professional caregivers, and support groups that can provide the necessary assistance. Explore these options and find what works best for your situation.

In maintaining independence, setting boundaries and expressing preferences is equally important. Accepting help does not mean relinquishing control over your life. It's about making informed choices and directing the type of assistance you want to receive. Doing so allows you to continue leading a life that aligns with your values and desires.

Asking for help is proof of the resilience and adaptability that comes with aging. It's about recognizing the changes in our abilities and adjusting our approach to self-care accordingly. By balancing independence with the proper support, we can continue to live fulfilling lives, moving through our golden years with confidence and respect.

Chapter Summary

- Self-care is an essential part of aging with grace, encompassing personal hygiene, nutrition, physical activity, rest, mental and emotional care, and healthcare management.
- Personal hygiene, including bathing and oral care, boosts confidence and health. At the same time, nutrition may need to be adjusted with age to maintain energy and health.

- Regular physical activity is crucial for maintaining flexibility, strength, balance, and mental health, and quality sleep is restorative for the body and mind.
- Mental and emotional well-being involves stimulating the brain and maintaining social connections while managing healthcare, including proactive medical appointments and treatments.
- Mobility aids and home adaptations, such as ramps and grab bars, can enhance independence, and smart home devices can ease household tasks.
- Personal safety in the home is vital, involving clear pathways, adequate lighting, emergency response systems, and a support network.
- Responsible medication management requires understanding, organization, adherence, monitoring for side effects, and regular reviews with healthcare providers.
- Asking for help is a strength, not a weakness. It involves acknowledging when support is needed, understanding your needs, and finding the right balance of resources and independence.

7

LEISURE AND EXPLORING NEW HORIZONS IN RETIREMENT

As we enter retirement, life offers a range of opportunities, encouraging us to fill our days with the excitement of exploration and learning. Travel at this time isn't just about seeing new places; it's a deep dive into the world's wide variety of cultures, environments, and histories.

Traveling in retirement celebrates the freedom earned after years of hard work, offering a break from the usual and a chance to experience new things. It is an opportunity to step out of the familiar, challenge the mind, and enrich the soul. For many, it's the fulfillment of a long-held dream, an opportunity to see the places they've always wanted to visit that have quietly called to them.

Travel is also a unique chance to reconnect with yourself and your loved ones. It can be a solitary pilgrimage to places with personal significance or a group adventure with family and friends, creating memories that will be cherished for years. It is a time to forge new friendships with people from all walks of life, share stories and laughter, and learn from the collective wisdom of diverse cultures.

The beauty of travel at this stage is the luxury of time. Without the constraints of limited vacation days, you can immerse yourself fully in the experience, whether lingering in a museum to absorb every detail, taking the long route to savor the landscape, or sitting at a café and watching the world go by. This is the time to take things slowly, be present in the moment, and appreciate the small details that a rushed journey might overlook.

Travel can be tailored to the comfort and pace that suits your lifestyle and needs. Many options are available, from leisurely river cruises to guided tours that take care of all the details, allowing travelers to enjoy their adventures without stress or strain.

Travel can also be an enriching conduit for learning and growth. It challenges you to step out of your comfort zone, navigate new languages, taste unfamiliar cuisines, and understand different ways of life. It is an active engagement with the world that keeps the mind sharp and the spirit young.

Exploring hobbies in retirement adds another layer of life satisfaction. While travel broadens our external horizons, hobbies encourage us to look inside ourselves, discovering new aspects of who we are and new paths to happiness and creativity.

Hobbies: The Joy of Personal Passions

In our golden years, we find ourselves with limitless time and a desire for fulfillment. Engaging in hobbies that bring us joy and fuel our passions is an essential part of our overall happiness and health.

Hobbies offer a unique blend of pleasure and purpose, a combination that is especially meaningful during retirement. They allow us to express ourselves, learn and grow, and connect with others on a level that transcends the mundane. Whether it's the delicate art of painting, the rhythmic pleasure of knitting, the challenge of chess, or the physical satisfaction of gardening, hobbies provide a canvas for our creativity and a playground for our intellect.

The beauty of personal passions comes from their variety and the unique significance they have for each person. For some, collecting antiques or stamps offers a connection to history and a sense of continuity. For others, photography captures the fleeting beauty of the world around us, freezing moments in time to be cherished forever.

Engaging in hobbies also has a profound impact on our health. Studies have shown that staying mentally and physically active can lead to a longer and more satisfying life. The concentration required to master a new skill can improve cognitive function, while the social interaction often accompanying hobby groups can ward off loneliness and depression.

Hobbies can also be a form of legacy, a way to share our knowledge and passions with younger generations. The recipes perfected over a lifetime, woodwork crafted with skilled hands, or quilt that weaves together the fabric of family history are gifts that carry a part of ourselves into the future.

Hobbies enrich our lives in numerous ways. Commitment to a hobby can lead to expertise, provide personal fulfillment, and earn the respect and admiration of others. Retirement's flexibility lets us discover new interests or reawaken past passions, reigniting the excitement we felt in our younger days.

Hobbies add color, texture, and pattern to our lives. They remind us that, at any age, happiness can be found in the pursuit of personal passions.

Volunteering: Giving Back with Time and Talent

After exploring the rich satisfaction that hobbies can provide, it's worth considering another avenue of fulfillment that enriches the self and the broader community: volunteering.

Volunteering is a powerful way to give back, a gesture of gratitude, and an act that shows that every individual can make a difference. It's about sharing the most valuable assets one possesses – time and talent – to create positive change. As we age, volunteering offers a unique opportunity to apply a lifetime of skills and knowledge in new, meaningful ways.

The beauty of volunteering lies in its diversity. Opportunities arise in various sectors, including education, healthcare, environmental conservation, and the arts. You might find fulfillment in mentoring young people, bringing your professional expertise to nonprofit organizations, or providing companionship to those in need.

Volunteering has a symbiotic nature. While the main goal is to contribute to the welfare of others, volunteers often find that they receive as much as they give. The social interaction and sense of purpose you can get from volunteering can combat loneliness and depression, common concerns in later life. It can also provide a sense of structure and routine that some people miss after leaving the workforce.

In addition to the emotional and psychological benefits, there's evidence to suggest that volunteering can positively affect physical health. Engaging with others and staying active in a volunteer role can help maintain mental acuity, physical stamina, and overall well-being.

Giving back through volunteering is both a service to the community and a gift to yourself. It's a way to remain connected, continue growing, and acknowledge that no matter your age, there are always new ways to contribute and new joys to discover.

Gardening: The Therapeutic Touch of Nature

As the sun rises, casting a warm glow over soft petals and dewy leaves, a sense of peace and anticipation fills the air. Gardening is a celebration of life, growth, and continual renewal. It's a hobby that combines the beauty of nature with the nurturing touch of our hands, creating a sanctuary where time slows down and the soul is nourished.

For many, gardening is a therapeutic ritual. The feel of soil between your fingers, the careful tending to a budding plant, and watching it flourish can be deeply rewarding. Gardening showcases the virtues of patience and the benefits of careful nurturing. In our later years, it provides a perfect mix of exercise and leisure, a balance crucial if we want to age gracefully.

The garden is a canvas for creativity and expression. Choosing which seeds to plant, designing the layout of a flowerbed, or pairing vegetables and herbs that will grow in harmony all contribute to a sense of purpose and fulfillment. The colors, textures, and fragrances of a garden can be a source of immense pleasure, stimulating the senses in a calming and invigorating way.

Gardening encourages us to connect with the cycles of nature. It teaches us to accept the impermanent nature of life as seasons change and plants go through their life cycles. There's a lesson in witnessing the first sprouts of spring, the abundance of summer, the harvests of autumn, and the quiet dormancy of winter. Each season has its beauty and role in the grand cycle of life.

There are also numerous health benefits of gardening. It's a gentle exercise that can improve endurance, flexibility, and strength. Tasks like digging, planting, weeding, and watering contribute to maintaining physical health without the strain of high-impact activities. Additionally, exposure to sunlight provides essential vitamin D, which is vital for bone health and immune function.

Gardening also offers an opportunity for social interaction and community building. Sharing cuttings, exchanging tips with fellow gardeners, or simply enjoying the company of others in a community garden can lead to meaningful relationships and a sense of belonging. It's a way to stay engaged with others, share in the fruits of harvest, and support each other through nature's challenges.

For those who may not have access to a garden, container gardening is a wonderful alternative. It allows the cultivation of herbs, flowers, and even some vegetables from the comfort of a balcony or windowsill. This adaptability ensures that the therapeutic touch of nature is within reach for everyone, regardless of where they live.

In the tranquility of the garden, there is a space for reflection and meditation. It's a place where the world's worries can be set aside, and the focus can shift to the simple, grounding tasks at hand. Gardening is a reminder that growth and change are constants. As we cultivate our gardens, we also cultivate our well-being, finding joy in the rhythm of nature and the simple act of nurturing life.

Games and Recreation: Fun as a Fountain of Youth

In retirement, seeking leisure and fun is an essential part of a lively and satisfying life. Games and recreation aren't just for children; they're like a source of youthfulness, helping to keep our minds and bodies agile and spirited.

Games offer a unique blend of mental stimulation and social interaction that can be particularly beneficial as we age. Board games, card games, and even digital games can sharpen cognitive skills, enhance memory, and foster problem-solving abilities. Engaging in these playful challenges can be a great way to keep the brain active and engaged and help ward off the mental fog that sometimes accompanies aging.

Recreational activities like bowling, dancing, or even participating in a local theater production can provide physical exercise and a sense of community and belonging. These activities encourage us to step out of our comfort zones, learn new skills, and connect with others, all of which are essential for aging gracefully.

Laughter and joy that inherently come with games and recreation are powerful antidotes to stress and loneliness. They remind us that life can be filled with fun and playfulness at any age. In these times of fun and friendship, we often discover the strongest bonds with our friends, family, and even within ourselves.

If you integrate games and recreational activities into your daily routine, you'll discover that they are more than simply a way to pass the time. They celebrate life's continued potential for growth, learning, and happiness. They are a way to embrace fun as a fundamental part of our lives. Through these different experiences, we continue to evolve, proving that we are all young at heart, no matter our age.

Chapter Summary

- Retirement offers the opportunity to travel, providing a meaningful engagement with diverse cultures and the freedom to explore long-held dreams. It allows us to reconnect with ourselves and loved ones, creating cherished memories and new friendships.
- Hobbies are a source of joy and self-expression, offering a chance to pursue personal passions and stay

mentally and physically active. Engaging in hobbies can improve health, provide a sense of purpose, and allow us to leave a legacy through shared knowledge and skills.
- Volunteering during retirement enables us to give back to the community, utilizing our time and talents in meaningful ways. It offers emotional, psychological, and physical health benefits, fostering social connections and a sense of purpose.
- Gardening can provide therapeutic benefits, physical activity, and a connection to nature, contributing to overall well-being and community engagement.
- Games and recreational activities in later years promote mental agility, social interaction, and physical activity, enhancing quality of life and fostering a youthful spirit.

8

HEALTH CHALLENGES AND MEDICAL CARE

As we age, figuring out the healthcare system is like navigating a new terrain with an intricate map. The prospect can be daunting at first, but with the right knowledge and support, it can also be a journey to maintaining and enhancing our quality of life.

Understanding the healthcare system is crucial because it is the gateway to receiving the medical care and support we need. This system is more than just a collection of doctors and hospitals; it's a complex network of insurance plans, pharmacies, specialists, and home health services, all of which are there to help us stay on top of our health as we age.

One of the first steps in navigating this system with ease is to establish a strong relationship with a primary care physician. This doctor will become your main point of contact, helping to coordinate care and make informed decisions about your health. They are the ones who know your medical history, understand your concerns, and can help you out when specialists or additional services are needed.

We often find ourselves managing multiple prescriptions with age. It can be helpful to have a pharmacist you trust to discuss your medications, their possible side effects, and how they interact. A good pharmacist can be a valuable resource, offering advice on medication management and ensuring that your treatment plan is safe and effective.

Insurance is another aspect of the healthcare system that can be particularly complex. Understanding your coverage, what it entails, and how to maximize your benefits is a skill that will serve you well. Don't hesitate to ask questions or seek assistance from insurance representatives or patient advocacy groups to clarify your entitlements and responsibilities.

Technology has also become a significant part of healthcare management. From online patient portals that allow you to access your medical records to telehealth services that enable you to consult with doctors virtually, don't be afraid to embrace these tools. They can simplify managing appointments, refilling prescriptions, and keeping track of your health.

Support groups and community services can offer invaluable assistance. These groups provide practical advice and assistance as well as emotional support from others who understand the challenges of aging. Whether it's help with transportation to medical appointments or navigating health-related paperwork, these organizations can be a lifeline.

Lastly, remember that you are not alone on this journey. Family, friends, and caregivers can be integral in helping you manage your healthcare needs. They can accompany you to appointments, help you manage medication, or be there to listen when you're feeling overwhelmed.

Navigating the healthcare system as we age can be challenging but can be met with grace and determination. By building a network of trusted professionals, staying informed, and getting support when needed, we can take control of our health and continue to live life to the fullest.

Chronic Conditions: Managing Long-Term Health Issues

Chronic health conditions can often feel like an unwelcome companion on our path through life. These long-term health issues, which may include arthritis, hypertension, diabetes, heart disease, and osteoporosis, among others, are conditions that we need to understand and handle with patience and kindness.

Managing chronic conditions involves balancing medical advice with personal lifestyle choices. It begins with a comprehensive understanding of each condition, its potential complications, and available treatments. Knowledge is empowering; when armed with the right information, you can make informed decisions about your health care.

Regular check-ups and open communication with doctors can help monitor the progress of these conditions and adjust treatments if needed. It is important to ask questions, express your concerns, and discuss any side effects of medications or therapies. Remember, you are the most important member of your healthcare team, and your insights into your body's responses are invaluable.

Lifestyle modifications also play a significant role in managing chronic conditions. A balanced diet, regular physical activity, and adequate rest are foundational to maintaining health and vitality. Nutritional needs can change with age, so it may be beneficial to consult with a dietitian to ensure that your diet supports your health conditions. Similarly, appropriate exercise can help manage symptoms and improve overall well-being. Even gentle activities like walking, swimming, or tai chi can make a significant difference.

Emotional support is just as important as physical care. Chronic conditions can sometimes lead to feelings of frustration, isolation, or sadness. Seek support from friends, family, or support groups where experiences and coping strategies can be shared. Remember, you are not alone on this journey, and sharing your story can provide comfort and offer others insights.

Aging with grace while managing chronic conditions is about embracing each day with optimism and resilience. It's about making informed choices, seeking joy in the everyday, and recognizing the beauty in the wisdom that comes with experience.

Mental Health Concerns: Addressing Depression and Anxiety

We've already explored the importance of looking after our bodies and minds. Our lives are full of experiences, but sometimes, as we age, we might start to struggle with our mental health, facing challenges like depression and anxiety. These aren't just small worries that come and go; they're bigger issues that can impact how happy and comfortable we feel every day. We should take these concerns seriously and treat them with as much care and kindness as a physical illness.

Depression in the later stages of life is often misinterpreted as a natural part of aging, but this is not always true. Depression is not an inevitable consequence of growing older but a medical condition that can and should be treated. The symptoms may be subtle or mistakenly attributed to other health issues or life changes, such as losing loved ones, retirement, or physical decline. However, it can significantly impact one's sense of joy, energy, and purpose, which can be immense.

Similarly, anxiety can be a silent but heavy burden, making us worry about health, financial security, and the well-being of family members. It can manifest as a constant sense of nervousness, trouble sleeping, or feeling overwhelmed by small, everyday tasks.

The first step in addressing these mental health concerns is recognition. We need to listen to ourselves with the same empathy we offer others. Acknowledging feelings of sadness, worry, or fear is an act of courage, not a sign of weakness. Have open conversations with healthcare providers, who can offer screenings and referrals to mental health professionals if needed.

Treatment for depression and anxiety can take many forms, and each person may face it differently. Medication can be an effective tool, but it is often most beneficial when combined with other therapies. Counseling or psychotherapy provides a space to explore feelings and develop coping strategies. Cognitive-behavioral therapy, in particular, has shown promise in helping older adults reframe negative thought patterns that contribute to depression and anxiety.

Beyond clinical interventions, there are everyday actions that can boost your mental health. Maintaining social connections, engaging in physical activity if your health permits, and cultivating hobbies and interests can all play a role in lifting spirits and reducing anxiety. Mindfulness practices, such as meditation or deep-breathing exercises, can also be powerful allies in the quest for mental tranquility.

It's also important to consider the environment in which one ages. A supportive community, whether family, friends, or a dedicated senior living arrangement, can provide the social stimulation and sense of belonging that are vital to mental health. Access to resources such as senior centers, support groups, and educational workshops can empower older adults to take charge of their mental well-being.

Mental health is not a destination but a continuous path we walk, with its own set of challenges and triumphs. By addressing conditions like depression and anxiety with the same care we give to physical illnesses, we honor the full spectrum of our health and embrace the possibility of a life lived with happiness and resilience.

Rehabilitation and Recovery: Bouncing Back from Illness

Our strength and spirit are often tested by the health challenges that come with age. No one wants illness, but it doesn't have to be a permanent resident in our lives. The road to recovery, though sometimes tough and full of twists and turns, is paved with the promise of rehabilitation and the chance of returning to a life of purpose and happiness.

Rehabilitation, often associated with strength and renewal, is vital to the healing process. It is the bridge that carries us from sickness to health. For older people, it's not only about physical recovery. It's about reclaiming independence, maintaining self-respect, and making their lives more enjoyable.

The process of rehabilitation and recovery is different for everyone. It usually starts with a comprehensive assessment by healthcare professionals who understand the situation. This team could include physicians, nurses, physical therapists, occupational therapists, speech therapists, and social workers, all working together to tailor a recovery plan that respects the individual's goals and limitations.

Physical therapy is crucial in helping us regain strength, balance, and mobility in our later years. It provides the adage that movement is medicine. Through guided exercises and encouragement, physical therapists help individuals rebuild the physical abilities that may have been eroded by illness. On the other hand, occupational therapy focuses on the practical aspects of daily living, ensuring that individuals can navigate their environments safely and perform the tasks that bring meaning to their lives.

Speech therapy is also an essential part of the recovery process for those facing neurological events or other communication conditions. The ability to express oneself and engage in conversation is a cornerstone of human connection, and speech therapists work diligently to restore this critical aspect of interaction.

The emotional and psychological dimensions of recovery are equally important. Returning to good health can be overloaded with frustration, fear, and uncertainty. Here, the compassionate support of mental health professionals and loved ones becomes invaluable, helping support the spirit as the body heals.

Rehabilitation thrives on the support system surrounding the individual—family, friends, and caregivers offering their presence as a source of comfort and motivation. Their involvement is often the catalyst that propels recovery forward, transforming the rehabilitation experience into a shared journey.

Technology has brought new dimensions to rehabilitation, with innovative tools and devices enhancing the therapeutic experience. From telemedicine consultations to advanced equipment that aids in physical therapy, technology has become a powerful tool in the journey to recovery.

As individuals progress through rehabilitation, it is essential to celebrate each milestone, no matter how small. These victories are the stepping stones that lead to a fuller, more active life. They are reminders that every effort invested in recovery shows the enduring strength of the human spirit.

The determination to recover and the support of a caring community ultimately guide us back to the rhythm of life. The path of rehabilitation and recovery is one of transformation, where each step taken is closer to regaining the independence and well-being that enables us to live life to the fullest.

End-of-Life Care: Understanding Your Options

At some point in our lives, we are confronted with the reality that life is a cycle with a beginning and an end. Accepting this cycle with grace means acknowledging and preparing for the final stage of life. End-of-life care is a sensitive and important topic that deserves our attention and understanding. It includes the medical and emotional support provided during the period leading up to death. The goal is to make sure they are comfortable, their choices are respected, and their life is as good as it can be during this time.

Understanding your options for end-of-life care is an act of compassion for your loved ones. It involves making decisions that may be difficult but are essential in ensuring that your values and desires are honored. One of the primary options to consider is hospice care, which is designed to offer a supportive environment for individuals in the final phases of a terminal illness. Hospice care prioritizes pain management and emotional support, providing services at home, a hospice center, or a hospital.

Palliative care is another option that focuses on providing relief from the symptoms and stress of a severe illness. The goal is to improve the patients' and families' quality of life. Palliative care can be provided alongside curative treatments and is not limited to those at the end of life.

As we explored earlier, advance directives are legal documents that allow you to outline your preferences for end-of-life care before you cannot communicate them. These include a living will, which specifies the types of medical treatment you wish to receive or avoid, and a power of attorney for health care, which designates a person to make decisions on your behalf if you are unable to.

The conversation about end-of-life care is a very personal one. It involves discussing your wishes with family and healthcare providers, ensuring everyone understands your values and preferences. These discussions can provide peace of mind for you and your loved ones, knowing that your choices will be respected.

It's also essential to consider the emotional and spiritual aspects of end-of-life care. Many find comfort in counseling, spiritual guidance, or simply the presence of family and friends. Creating a peaceful environment, filled with personal touches like favorite music or cherished photographs, can also be a part of this final chapter.

In navigating these choices, seek healthcare professionals experienced in end-of-life care who can provide the guidance and support you need. They can help you understand the implications of different care options and help coordinate the various aspects of end-of-life care.

Chapter Summary

- The healthcare system can seem daunting at times, involving doctors, insurance, pharmacies, and home health services. Establishing a relationship with a primary care physician can help you coordinate your care and make health decisions.
- Trusting pharmacists can help manage medications and understand their interactions and side effects.
- Understanding insurance coverage and benefits is crucial; technology can help manage health records and appointments.
- Family, friends, and caregivers are vital in assisting with healthcare management, while support groups and community services can provide additional practical and emotional support as we age.
- Managing chronic conditions involves understanding the conditions, working with healthcare providers, and making lifestyle changes that suit you.
- Addressing mental health, such as depression and anxiety, is just as important as dealing with physical

illness. Treatments for mental health conditions include medication, therapy, and social support.
- End-of-life care is a sensitive and important topic that deserves attention and understanding. It includes the medical and emotional support provided during the period leading up to death and discussing your wishes with family and healthcare providers to ensure everyone understands your values and preferences.

9

THE DIGITAL AGE: STAYING CONNECTED AND INFORMED

The ways we connect with others and learn new things get more complex and colorful as technology advances. The internet, a vast and ever-expanding digital universe, offers many resources that can enrich our lives in countless ways. The internet is a way to connect to the wider world, a library of endless knowledge, and a space to share our stories and experiences.

From the comfort of your home, you can access a world of

resources to help you stay informed, learn new skills, and even manage your daily life more easily. Online banking, for instance, simplifies the way we handle our finances, allowing us to pay bills and monitor our accounts without the need to queue at the bank. Health portals provide valuable insights into wellness and medical information, empowering us to take charge of our health with informed decisions.

Online courses and tutorials allow us to learn anything, no matter where we are. Whether picking up a new language, exploring the mysteries of the universe, or delving into the arts, the internet is an ever-present mentor ready to guide you through your learning journey. It is a place where the mind can remain sharp and engaged, and the pursuit of knowledge continues to kindle the spirit of lifelong learning.

The internet is also a treasure trove of entertainment and leisure. Streaming services bring the thrill of cinema and television series into our living rooms, offering an escape to other worlds and stories. E-books and audiobooks provide a refuge for book lovers, ensuring that the joy of reading is only a click away.

Navigating this digital realm may seem scary initially, but with patience and a willingness to learn, it becomes a rewarding extension of one's living space. Approach the internet with a sense of adventure and openness, balanced with a healthy awareness of online safety and privacy. By setting strong passwords, understanding the basics of internet security, and being careful about the information we share, we can navigate the digital world safely and with confidence.

As we embrace the internet's vast offerings, we find that it keeps us connected not only to the world but also to our evolving selves. It fulfills the human need for growth and adaptation, proving that no matter our age, we can continue to expand our horizons and enrich our lives with the resources at our fingertips.

Social Media: Keeping in Touch with Loved Ones

Social media, often perceived as the young's playground, can also be a sanctuary for us as we navigate the golden years. It is a bridge across generations, a meeting place where grandparents can witness the milestones of their grandchildren, old friends can reunite with the ease of a click, and wisdom can be shared with the world.

The beauty of social media lies in its ability to adapt to our needs. For those who have watched the world evolve and seen the birth of television and the rise of the internet, social media is not just another technological leap; it is a tool that can be molded to fit the contours of their lives. It allows the sharing of stories, the celebration of anniversaries, and the comfort of seeing a loved one's face, even if they are miles away.

Engaging with these platforms can be as straightforward or as involved as one desires. You can start by creating a profile on a platform that resonates with you, be it the visual stories of Instagram, the community conversations of Facebook, or the rapid-fire updates of Twitter. Approach these spaces with curiosity and an open heart.

Privacy and comfort are paramount, and social media can be tailored to respect these boundaries. Customizing privacy settings ensures you share your life with those you trust, creating a safe space to express yourself. It's also a place to listen, learn from the experiences of others, and engage in the global dialogue that shapes our world.

If you're worried about the complexities of these platforms, fear not. The intuitive design of most social media sites makes them accessible, and there is always help at hand, be it from family, friends, or the platforms' support systems. The initial steps into this digital realm can be taken slowly, and with each venture, confidence grows. It's not about keeping pace with the changing algorithms or the latest trends; it's about finding a rhythm that suits your beat.

As we age, the desire to remain part of the community, to be involved and informed, continues. Social media offers that continuity, ensuring the world does not drift away as the years pass. It is both a window to the world and a mirror reflecting the life you've lived and the life you continue to live.

In this digital age, aging with grace includes embracing the tools that allow us to stay connected and informed. If you wish, carry the essence of who you are into the virtual realm and find joy in the new ways you can remain interwoven in those around you. As we continue our journey through the chapters of life, remember that the heart does not grow old. Its beat can be heard through social media across the vast expanse of the digital world.

Online Security: Protecting Yourself in the Digital World

Embracing the digital world brings a wealth of opportunities to stay connected and informed. However, as we navigate this ever-evolving landscape, we must be vigilant about our online security. While a tool of immense utility, the internet can also be a playground for those with less than honorable intentions. As we age, protecting our digital presence becomes even more critical to safeguard our personal information and ensure that our online experiences remain positive and enriching.

First and foremost, understand the basics of online security. This begins with the creation of strong, unique passwords for each of your accounts. A strong password is like a sturdy lock on the door of your online home; it should be complex, including a mix of letters, numbers, and symbols, and it should be changed regularly. Consider using a reputable password manager to keep track of your passwords, as this can alleviate the burden of memorization while maintaining a high level of security.

Another key aspect of online security is recognizing and avoiding phishing attempts. Phishing is a deceptive practice where scammers send emails or messages that appear to be from legitimate sources, such as your bank or a familiar service provider, to trick you into revealing sensitive information. Always be cautious with emails requesting personal details or urging you to click on unfamiliar links. When in doubt, contact the company directly using a phone number or website address you trust.

Updating your software is another simple yet effective step in protecting yourself online. Updates often include security patches that close vulnerabilities in your software, making it harder for hackers to access your system. Set your devices to update automatically, or make it a habit to check for updates regularly.

Socializing online can be a delightful way to keep in touch with friends and family, but it's important to manage your privacy settings on social media platforms. Customize who can see your posts and personal information. Be selective about what you share, and remember that the internet has a long memory; once something is posted, it can be difficult to erase.

Lastly, consider using two-factor authentication wherever possible. This adds an extra layer of security by requiring a second form of verification, such as a code sent to your phone, in addition to your password. This means that even if someone were to discover your password, they would still need this second code to access your account.

Taking these precautions can reduce the risk of falling victim to online threats. Staying informed about the latest security measures is as important as staying connected.

Smart Devices: Simplifying Daily Tasks

Embracing technology can enhance daily living rather than complicate it. Smart devices, with their intuitive interfaces and customizable features, offer many ways to simplify the tasks that once demanded more of our time and physical effort.

Imagine a morning that begins not with the arduous task of wrestling with appliance manuals or the physical strain of reaching high shelves but with a simple voice command that brews your coffee, adjusts the thermostat, or even reminds you to take your medication. This is the world smart devices have ushered in, where aging does not equate to losing independence or comfort.

The beauty of these devices lies in their ability to learn and adapt to our routines and preferences. A smart refrigerator can keep track of groceries and suggest shopping lists, while a smart oven can ensure that meals are cooked to perfection with minimal supervision. Gadgets like these are companions in the kitchen, helping us maintain a healthy and balanced diet, which becomes increasingly important as we age.

Beyond the kitchen, smart devices extend their reach to safety and security. Motion sensors and automated alerts provide peace of mind. The ability to monitor one's home remotely means that help is always within reach, and independence does not come at the cost of security.

The integration of smart technology into the home environment also fosters social connections. Video calling allows for face-to-face conversations with family and friends, bridging the gap that physical distance may create. It's a poignant reminder that the warmth of a smile or the comfort of a familiar face is only a few taps away.

Smart devices can also be used for personal growth and mental stimulation. They offer access to audiobooks, music, and podcasts, all of which can be enjoyed without fiddling with complex controls or small buttons. Keeping our minds active and learning new things is always important, no matter how old we are. Smart technology helps ensure that age doesn't stop us from continuing to learn and grow.

If you choose to integrate smart devices into your life, approach them with a sense of curiosity and patience. There is a learning curve, but it can be navigated with support and guidance. Many communities offer workshops and classes designed to help seniors become more comfortable with technology, and a growing number of resources are available online.

Aging with grace in the digital age is about balancing embracing new technologies and maintaining the essence of what makes life meaningful. Smart devices are tools, and when used thoughtfully, they can enhance our ability to live with meaning and connection.

E-Learning: Opportunities for Continued Education

The pursuit of knowledge keeps our lives full of fulfillment and activity. The digital age has opened up a treasure trove of opportunities for continued education that we might not have had before. Online learning, or E-learning, is a remarkable tool that empowers us to learn, grow, and thrive, regardless of our age.

Gone are the days when learning was confined to the four walls of a classroom or the pages of a textbook. Today, the world is our classroom, and the internet is our teacher, offering various courses, workshops, and seminars that cater to different interests and needs. Whether it's delving into the mysteries of ancient history, mastering a new language, or exploring the wonders of digital photography, e-learning platforms provide an accessible and flexible way to continue our education at our own pace and comfort.

For those of us who have witnessed the evolution of technology over the decades, the idea of online learning may initially seem intimidating. However, these platforms are designed with user-friendliness in mind. Many offer step-by-step tutorials and support systems to guide users through the process, ensuring that even those new to digital devices can easily navigate the learning environment.

E-learning is also about connecting with others who share our interests and passions. Virtual classrooms and forums create communities of learners, enabling us to engage in meaningful discussions, exchange ideas, and forge friendships that enrich our lives beyond the screen. This sense of community can be precious as we age, providing social interaction and intellectual stimulation that contribute to our well-being.

E-learning can be a source of empowerment and confidence. As we complete courses and gain new skills, we reinforce the understanding that age is not a barrier to learning. This can profoundly impact our self-esteem and perception of what it means to age with grace. It reminds us that our capacity for growth and adaptation is not diminished by the years we have lived but enhanced by the wisdom we have gained.

In embracing the opportunities for continued education that e-learning offers, we also set an example for future generations. We demonstrate that learning is a lifelong journey that enriches our lives and keeps us connected to the ever-evolving world around us.

Chapter Summary

- The internet provides a wealth of resources for all ages, acting as a bridge to the wider world and a source of endless knowledge.

- Thanks to the digital world, we can engage in lifelong learning through online courses and tutorials, exploring new subjects and keeping our minds sharp.
- The internet offers entertainment options like streaming services, e-books, and audiobooks, providing leisure and relaxation at home. However, the internet should be approached openly and cautiously, ensuring online safety through strong passwords and privacy awareness.
- Social media allows us to stay connected with loved ones, share experiences, and participate in global conversations.
- Smart devices can simplify daily tasks, enhancing safety, comfort, and social connections.

10

AGING IN PLACE: MAKING THE MOST OF YOUR HOME

As we journey through the golden years of our lives, the familiar comfort of our homes becomes even more important to us. Within these walls, we have celebrated life's milestones, weathered tough times, and found peace in the quiet moments. Aging with grace means being able to adapt, and adapting our homes to meet our changing needs is a powerful way to look after ourselves.

Home modifications for safety and comfort affirm our desire to live life to its fullest, regardless of age. These modifications can range from simple additions to more extensive renovations, each to create an environment that is as safe as it is nurturing. Revisit the 'Art of Adaptation' chapter to learn how to modify your home to make your living spaces more manageable as you age.

These home modifications help prevent harm and enhance quality of life. They allow us to continue engaging with our passions, welcome family and friends, and live with autonomy.

Community Resources and Support Services

In old age, we may feel an increasing desire to remain in the familiar comfort of our homes. Aging in place is a choice many make, and it can be richly rewarding with suitable support systems in place. Beyond the physical modifications to our homes discussed earlier, a robust network of community resources and support services is pivotal in enabling this independence.

Community resources come in various forms, from local senior centers that offer socialization and recreational activities to meal delivery services that ensure proper nutrition when cooking becomes a challenge.

Transportation services, too, are an integral component of community support. They provide the means for individuals to maintain their autonomy to attend medical appointments, shop for groceries, or enjoy a change of scenery without the stress of driving. These services often include reduced fares or even door-to-door assistance for those with mobility issues.

Another invaluable resource is legal and financial counseling. As we age, navigating the complexities of estate planning, healthcare directives, and benefits can be overwhelming. Community-based programs often offer workshops or one-on-one counseling to help seniors confidently understand their rights and plan for the future.

Health and wellness programs tailored to the needs of older adults are also a cornerstone of community support. These may include exercise classes to maintain mobility and balance, health screenings, and educational seminars on managing chronic conditions.

Community resources and support services provide the practical assistance, emotional support, and sense of connection essential for a fulfilling and independent life at home. As we move forward, we will explore another type of support for those who wish to age in place: in-home care options.

In-Home Care: Options for Assistance

In-home care is a helpful source of help as we age, providing various services to match different needs and wants.

It is a compassionate way to balance the desire for autonomy with the help we might need, ensuring we stay safe, have company, and are well taken care of.

Personal care assistants, sometimes known as aides, can help us when we may not be as steady as they once were. They can assist with the daily rituals of living, like bathing, dressing, and grooming. For many, these tasks are intimate, and the presence of a gentle and respectful assistant can make all the difference in preserving dignity and comfort.

Healthcare at home is not limited to non-medical aid. Registered and licensed practical nurses are available for those requiring medical attention, from medication management to wound care. Their expertise is not just in the procedures they perform but in their ability to provide reassurance and understanding to those under their care.

Meal preparation services are another component of in-home care. Whether it's due to dietary restrictions or the simple challenge of cooking for one, having someone to prepare wholesome, balanced meals can nourish the body as much as the soul.

Mobility and the freedom it brings can sometimes be hindered as we age. Physical and occupational therapists can visit homes to provide exercises and strategies to maintain or improve mobility, ensuring that the home remains a place of freedom, not confinement.

Companionship, often overlooked, is as crucial as any medical service. Loneliness can become more common as we age, but companion services offer light through shared activities, conversation, and the simple, profound presence of another person. This companionship can range from a few hours a week to live-in support.

Choosing the right type of in-home care is a deeply personal decision that should be made with careful consideration of your needs, values, and financial circumstances. It is a collaborative process involving family, healthcare providers, and the individuals providing the care. Open communication about expectations, boundaries, and the evolving nature of your needs is essential to creating a supportive and adaptive environment.

Aging in place with the support of in-home care is about crafting a life stage not defined by limitations but by the possibilities that thoughtful assistance can provide. It is about continuing to write one's story at home, surrounded by the memories that echo through the halls and the new ones waiting to be made.

Downsizing: Simplifying Your Surroundings

Downsizing, or simplifying your surroundings, can be a natural step in aging gracefully. It's a proactive approach to making your home more manageable and suited to your changing lifestyle.

Downsizing is not just about letting go of possessions; it's about curating your space to improve your quality of life. It involves a thoughtful paring down of belongings that allows for easier maintenance and accessibility. This simplification can lead to a safer living environment, reducing the risk of accidents and ensuring daily tasks are less strenuous.

The first step in this journey is to assess your current living situation. Take stock of the items you use regularly and those that have gone untouched for years. It's helpful to categorize belongings into essentials, sentimental items, and things that can be donated or discarded. Remember, the goal is to retain what adds value to your life and supports your daily routine.

When it comes to sentimental items, try to find a balance. These pieces are tangible connections to our past but need not overwhelm our present. Consider keeping only a select few with the deepest meaning or evoke the fondest memories. You might also explore creative ways to preserve memories, such as converting photos into digital formats or crafting a memory quilt from old clothing.

It's also worth considering the future when downsizing. What modifications might you need to make to your home to accommodate potential mobility changes? Planning for these adjustments now can make transitions smoother down the line.

Downsizing can be emotional, and taking it one step at a time is okay. It's an opportunity to set the stage for a new chapter of life that prioritizes ease, safety, and joy. Remember, the space you create doesn't just house you; it should reflect and support who you are at this stage of life.

Family, friends, and professionals can offer support and guidance throughout the process. They can help you make decisions, assist with the physical aspects of downsizing, and provide emotional support as you navigate this change.

Downsizing can pave the way for a home that continues to be a source of comfort and where you can age with grace and dignity. It's about making room in your home and your life for new experiences, relationships, and the peace that comes with a simplified, harmonious environment.

The Emotional Aspects of Aging in Place

Our homes are treasure chests full of memories, painting the picture of our lives. Every room is filled with the sounds of past laughter, the quiet of old talks, and the marks of memorable moments. These memories become a big part of who we are as we age. Growing old in our home keeps us tied to these stories, giving us a comforting sense of ongoing life. The walls around us become part of who we are, offering a warm hug in a world that always seems to be moving and shifting.

The choice to age in place also has unique emotional challenges. The passage of time may alter our relationship with our home. Rooms once filled with the energy of a bustling family may now stand quieter, prompting feelings of loneliness or loss. Maintaining a household that once seemed effortless can become a source of stress or frustration as our physical abilities shift.

If you begin to experience these feelings, sit with them and understand that they are a natural response to the changes that aging brings. Recognizing the resilience and adaptability that come with age is just as important. We learn to find new rhythms and create new routines that honor our current selves while staying true to the essence of our home.

To manage the emotional complexities of aging in place, it is beneficial to cultivate a supportive community, whether it be through neighbors, friends, family, or local services. Social connections can transform the experience of aging in place from one of isolation to one of engagement and purpose. Inviting others into our space for a cup of tea, a shared meal, or simply a chat can breathe new life into our homes and our hearts.

Personalizing your living space to reflect your current lifestyle and passions can reinvigorate your emotional bond with your home. This could mean converting a child's old bedroom into a space for a new hobby or interest or redesigning a living area to host gatherings for book clubs or game nights. By doing so, you can create an environment that accommodates your physical needs and nourishes your emotional well-being.

Aging in place is a journey that is as much about the heart as the home. It is about creating a sanctuary that shelters our aging bodies and cradles our evolving spirits.

Chapter Summary

- Aging in place involves adapting homes to meet changing needs and enhancing safety, comfort, and independence.
- Home modifications can include better lighting, slip-resistant flooring, bathroom grab bars, and accessible kitchen designs.
- Community resources and support services provide socialization, meal delivery, transportation, legal and financial counseling, and health programs as we age.
- In-home care options range from personal care assistants to medical professionals, offering services like

meal preparation, mobility assistance, and companionship.
- Downsizing involves simplifying living spaces by decluttering and reorganizing to improve safety and manageability.
- The emotional aspects of aging in place include maintaining a connection to personal history and adapting to changes in the home environment.
- Cultivating a supportive community and personalizing living spaces can help combat loneliness and enhance emotional well-being.
- Aging in place is a holistic approach that considers physical, emotional, and social needs to create a comfortable and meaningful living environment.

CLOSING THOUGHTS AND REFLECTIONS

As we walk the path of life, we collect a mosaic of experiences, each teaching us a lesson that adds to the wisdom we carry forward. When we reflect on our life's journey, especially during our later years, we see all the things we've learned and the elegance with which we've moved through our days.

One of the most significant lessons is the art of resilience. Life challenges our strength and flexibility in its unpredictable ebb and flow. Aging with grace teaches us that resilience is not about avoiding the storm but learning to dance in the rain. It's about finding happiness amid sorrow, strength in vulnerability, and growth in adversity.

Another lesson is the importance of relationships. The value of deep, meaningful connections becomes ever more apparent as the years pass. These relationships—be they with family, friends, or community members—form the foundation of our support system. They offer love, laughter, and comfort, reminding us that we are not solitary travelers but part of a rich narrative of human connection.

We also learn the lesson of letting go. With age comes the understanding that not everything in life can be controlled. Letting go of past wrongs, unmet expectations, and roads not taken frees us to live more fully in the present. It allows us to forgive ourselves and others, release the weight of what we cannot change, and cherish the moments that bring light to our days.

The journey teaches us about the beauty of simplicity. As the clutter of earlier decades falls away, the simple pleasures come into sharper focus. A cup of tea in the quiet of the morning, the laughter of our family, the comfort of a well-loved book—these simple joys become the highlights of our days, reminding us that happiness often resides in the smallest moments.

Lastly, aging with grace imparts the wisdom of gratitude. Each year, we become more acutely aware of life's fragility and the gift each day presents. Gratitude becomes a daily practice, a way of seeing the world that enriches our experience and fills us with peace and contentment.

As we reflect on these lessons, we realize that aging is both a physical process but a spiritual and emotional journey. It is a time to harvest the wisdom sown throughout our lives, share it with others, and prepare ourselves for the next chapter with an open heart and a spirit of anticipation. The journey, with all its twists and turns, has brought us to a place of introspection and understanding—a place where we can look back with appreciation and look forward with hope.

The Gift of Memories: Cherishing the Past

Our memories are the vibrant colors that give richness and depth to our lives. They are the narrative of our journey, a collection of moments, both big and small, that have shaped who we are. To age with grace is to cherish these memories and hold them close as treasured keepsakes.

Memories are more than just recollections of past events; they are the legacy of our emotions and experiences. They are the laughter that echoed through the halls of a childhood home, the warmth of a loved one's embrace, and the bittersweet tears of a farewell that was not the end but a transition. In our later years, these memories become integral to our identity, the stories we share with younger generations, and the wisdom we impart.

Cherishing the past does not mean living in it but rather honoring it. It is about acknowledging the struggles we've overcome, the love we've given and received, and the knowledge we've gained. It is about recognizing that every challenge faced and every joy embraced has contributed to the strength and resilience that characterizes a life well-lived.

As we age, we may find that our memories begin to fade, like the soft edges of an old photograph. However, this does not diminish their value. Instead, it invites us to revisit them, speak about them, and write them down, ensuring that they continue to live on for those who will follow in our footsteps.

The gift of memories is also a reminder of our shared humanity. It connects us to others, creating a connection that is not solely our own but part of a larger, more intricate network. Our stories intertwine with those of our friends, family, and even strangers, creating a narrative that spans time and space.

In this reflective space, we find comfort and joy in the memories we've cultivated. We understand that while our physical abilities may wane, the mind's garden of memories remains fertile, ready to be tended and appreciated.

In the calmness of our later years, when the hustle of life slows to a gentler pace, we have the precious opportunity to sift through these memories and find peace in knowing that our lives have been a collection of meaningful moments.

Embracing the Present: The Power of Now

The true art of aging with grace can be found in embracing the present. The present is a canvas upon which the colors of every yesterday and the light of each tomorrow blend into the masterpiece of now.

Living in the present means accepting the symphony of life with all its ups and downs. It means sitting in the garden of existence, inhaling the fragrance of blooming flowers without lamenting yesterday's fallen petals or wishing for tomorrow's buds.

The present is also a sanctuary of acceptance. It is where age is not a sign of wear but a badge of honor, reflecting the resilience and the stories etched in the lines of a well-lived life. Here, in the power of now, there is no need for the facades of youth because the beauty of the present is in the authenticity of the self, the comfort of one's skin, and the peace that comes with self-acceptance.

The present is where we can cultivate happiness and engage with the world around us with curiosity and wonder. It is where we can share the wisdom gleaned from years of experience, laugh with the innocence of a child, and impart the warmth of our spirit to those whose lives we touch.

Looking Forward: Hope and Aspirations

As we add the last details to our story of growing old gracefully, we look ahead to a future filled with hope and aspirations. It's like looking at the soft glow of the morning sun, hinting at the beginning of a new adventure even as we finish the current one.

In a life full of rich experiences, each event is a unique thread—a lesson, a treasured moment. As we age, these threads become interwoven with wisdom, resilience, and a deeper appreciation of the beauty of life. Our aspirations aren't just idle hopes; they are beacons that guide us, illuminating the path ahead with purpose and new opportunities.

Hope encourages us to picture a future where our wisdom enables us to contribute in ways we never thought possible. It is the gentle hand on our back that propels us forward, reminding us that our presence, stories, and insights are valuable gifts to the world around us.

As we look forward, we aspire to embody the grace we have cultivated. We think about sharing our narratives with younger generations, not as a blueprint for living but to show how one can navigate the waters of existence. We aspire to be mentors, friends, and confidants, offering our experiences as a lantern in the night for those who may find themselves lost in the shadows of uncertainty.

We seek to embrace the joy of living and find beauty in the simplicity of a morning's sunrise or the laughter of a loved one. We continue growing, learning, and loving with the fullness of our beings, for it is in these pursuits that we can find life's truest pleasures.

In the quiet moments of reflection, we may find ourselves

yearning for a sense of peace and contentment. This is the ultimate aspiration: to reach a place within ourselves where the bustle of life is met with a calm that comes from knowing we have lived authentically, loved deeply, and left a legacy of kindness and compassion.

We move forward with the understanding that each day is a precious opportunity to add another stroke of beauty to the masterpiece of our lives.

Your Graceful Path Forward

Let's take a moment to reflect on what it means to have aged gracefully. Aging with grace involves a daily commitment to embracing the beauty of our years and the wisdom that comes with it. It is a path we build with patience, kindness, and a deep appreciation for the little moments that make up our lives.

To age with grace is to understand that every wrinkle is a story, every gray hair a badge of honor, and every shared laugh a treasure. It means accepting the past without regret, living in the present with exhilaration, and approaching the future without fear.

Remember that you are alone on this journey. You are part of a community that has also journeyed through the seasons of life, each person with their unique narrative. Together, we can support and uplift one another, sharing the joys and shouldering the burdens that come over time.

Remember also that grace is not a static state but a dynamic process. It requires adaptability, an open heart, and a willingness to learn and grow. It asks that we remain curious, engaged, and connected to the world around us, never losing sight of the wonder life offers at every age.

In embracing this path forward, we acknowledge that the fullness of life is not diminished by age but rather enriched by it. We carry within us the pieces of every person we have loved, every challenge we have overcome, and every moment of beauty we have witnessed. These pieces connect to form the magnificent artwork of our existence, which is ever-evolving and uniquely ours.

As you continue to fill your canvas, do so with the understanding that aging is not a process of losing yourself but a continuous discovery of who you are meant to be. May your days be filled with purpose, your heart with compassion, and your life with the grace that comes from knowing you have lived well, loved deeply and left a legacy of poise and strength.

In the quiet moments of reflection, may you look upon your life with gentle pride and a new-found gratitude for the journey. Through the culmination of our years, we can truly understand the depth of our resilience, the power of our connections, and the beauty of a life well-lived.

EPILOGUE

I hope this book has ignited a spark within and inspired you to live life with greater purpose and clarity. Take some time to reflect on the path you have walked and ahead to the horizons yet to be explored. Together, we have embarked on a transformative expedition that has decluttered our physical spaces and cleared the way for a deeper, more meaningful engagement with life itself.

The essence of letting go and living well is not found in the grand gestures or monumental milestones but in the small, everyday decisions that shape our lives. It is in the book we pass on to a friend, knowing its pages hold laughter and solace. It is in the afternoon spent with old photographs, where memories dance in the light of our present. It is in the choice to learn something new, to embrace the day with curiosity and wonder, even as the years gather behind us.

As you close this book, may you carry forward the lessons of simplicity and vitality woven through its chapters. Let the practice of Swedish death cleaning inspire you to live with intention, to hold lightly to the material and tightly to the memories and relationships that truly enrich our lives. And let the guide to aging with grace shed light on the beauty of growing older, not as a time of decline but as an era of freedom, wisdom, and joy.

The journey does not end here. Each day offers a fresh canvas, a new opportunity to apply the principles of letting go and living well. There will be moments of challenge, of course—times when the clutter accumulates or when the weight of years feels heavy. In these moments, remember that the essence of this journey is not perfection but progress. It is about moving forward with compassion for ourselves and others, about making space for the new while honoring the past.

In the end, "How To Let Go and Live Well" is an invitation to view life through a lens of gratitude and grace. It is a call to cherish each moment, to embrace each season of life with open arms and an open heart. May this book be a stepping stone on your path to a lighter, more intentional future, and may you find the key to truly living well in the art of letting go.

Thank you for allowing this book to be a part of your journey. May the roads ahead be filled with discovery, peace, and an ever-deepening appreciation for the wonders of life.

YOUR FEEDBACK MATTERS

As we reach the end of this book, I extend my heartfelt gratitude for your time and engagement. It's been an honor to share this journey with you, and I hope it has been as enriching for you as it has been for me.

Your feedback helps me as an independent author and guides fellow readers searching for their next meaningful read. Your insights and reflections are invaluable; by sharing them, you contribute to a larger conversation that extends far beyond the pages of this book.

If the ideas we've explored have sparked new thoughts, inspired change, or provided comfort, I'd really appreciate it if you could share your experience with others by leaving a review on the platform on which you purchased this book.

Thank you once again for your company on this literary adventure. May the insights you've gained stay with you, and may your quest for knowledge be ever-fulfilling.

ABOUT THE AUTHOR

Hanna Bentsen is an expert in the art of mindful aging and intentional living. With a compassionate voice and a wealth of experience, her work revolutionizes the way we perceive aging and life's inevitable transitions and redefines the middle and later years as periods of growth and enrichment.

Her insightful explorations into Swedish Death Cleaning and the art of aging with grace challenge societal norms, encouraging readers to approach decluttering and aging with intention and dignity. Hanna's books empower readers to embrace the later stages of life with newfound purpose and vitality. They offer practical wisdom for decluttering life's physical and emotional spaces.

Hanna's love for Scandinavian culture, with its emphasis on simplicity and functionality, deeply influences her approach to a well-lived life.

www.ingramcontent.com/pod-product-compliance
Lightning Source LLC
Chambersburg PA
CBHW071339080526
44587CB00017B/2887